Rip Off the Big Game

PAUL HOCH is the author of three books published, or soon to be published, in England: *Academic Freedom in Action* (a study of the crisis in British universities); *LSE: The Natives Are Restless* (about the London School of Economics); and *The Newspaper Game*. Hoch, a theoretical physicist, is currently lecturing on the political sociology of sports at the Cambridge–Goddard Graduate School.

JACK SCOTT is the author of *The Athletic Revolution*. He is Athletic Director and Chairman of the Physical Education Department at Oberlin College and head of the Institute for the Study of Sport and Society, a center started as a clearinghouse for athletic abuses, from racial and sex discrimination to drug misuse.

RIP
OFF
THE
BIG
GAME:

THE
EXPLOITATION
OF SPORTS
BY THE POWER ELITE

by Paul Hoch

ANCHOR BOOKS

DOUBLEDAY & COMPANY, INC.

Garden City, New York

1972

Acknowledgments

The central themes of this book arose out of discussions between the author and his friends Bob Kellermann and Jane Wingate in England in 1970. Much of the preliminary research for the project was done by Kellermann. Judith Finlayson of the editorial staff of Doubleday of Canada was perhaps the first to recognize the worth of this work and provided badly needed encouragement toward its elaboration and completion, as well as several useful editorial suggestions. The manuscript was edited in a thorough and careful manner by Bill Whitehead, who provided so many useful editorial suggestions and insights that it is fair to say that the book would have been in a far less readable and polished state without his tireless efforts.

During the period in which the manuscript was being put into final shape the author enjoyed the hospitality of Jack and Micki Scott of the Institute for the Study of Sport and Society. The Scotts provided the author with many useful insights into the functioning of sports in this society, as well as a steady diet of valuable newspaper clippings on important day-to-day developments. The author also enjoyed the benefit of many extremely useful discussions with ex-National Football League players Dave Meggyesy, George Sauer, and Chip Oliver; track-and-field men like Bruce Kidd, Phil Shinnick, and Sammy Goldberg; and pro-basketball forward Bill Bradley. Also significant were the many discussions with college newspaper editors and sportswriters.

The author also derived much valuable information and perspective from the extremely useful and insightful, muckraking columns of Mike Jay of the New York *Daily World;* from such radical sports autobiographies as Dave Meggyesy's *Out of Their League,* Curt Flood's *The Way It Is,* and Bernie Parrish's *They Call It a*

Game. Jack Scott's book *The Athletic Revolution* provided a useful overview on the upheavals that are shaking the sports world. And Harry Edwards' book *The Revolt of the Black Athlete,* as well as the useful discussions the author enjoyed with Edwards himself, did much to shape an awareness of the racist core of too much of organized American sports.

It is customary in these acknowledgment sections to note that, though this book would not have been possible without the contributions of all these people and many more, the words and responsibility for the book are "mine and mine alone." While this may be true in a bourgeois legal sense, it is nevertheless a gross distortion of the truth. Behind every word of this book, behind every central theme and perspective that made such a book conceivable, stands the life and work of the man whose theoretical insights into the structure of mass culture under capitalism made this particular work possible. His name was Nino Gramsci. The author of the present work is virtually standing on his shoulders. Gramsci, in turn, stands on the shoulders of those even more towering figures of theoretical clarity and insight, V. I. Lenin and Karl Marx. It would be fairer to state that only *the errors* of the present work are "mine and mine alone." Whatever insights and perceptions it contains are the product, not of any one man (least of all, the present author), but of the entire world-wide, century-long movement for international socialism on a global scale. It is to that movement—and to the people of Vietnam who today stand in its forefront—that this volume is dedicated. Without that movement there would be no occasion, and no possibility, of writing anything.

Summer 1972   *Paul Hoch*

Contents

Introduction

by Jack Scott

The various ills of American sports have been aptly described during the past few years by journalists such as Leonard Shecter, Bob Lipsyte, Sandy Padwe, Ira Berkow, and a number of other courageous sportswriters who saw their work as something more than shilling for the sports establishment. On top of this criticism of the sports industry, we have recently seen athletes themselves become the sports establishment's most severe critics. A plethora of exposé books by ex-athletes have appeared in the last few years, ranging from the radical criticism of Dave Meggyesy in *Out of Their League* to the more moderate attack of Don Schollander in *Deep Water*.

The athlete as sports critic is a most significant development, for until recently nearly all prominent critics

of sports were academics or writers far removed from
the sports world. Not surprisingly, the criticism of these
outsiders was usually dismissed by people involved in
sports. Sportsmen—I consciously say men, for with few
rare exceptions women have been excluded from the
mainstream of American sports—viewed critics such as
Robert Hutchins and Thorstein Veblen as emaciated
academics who were simply upset by the physicality
of athletes. Coaches and athletes as well as most sports
fans also felt that most critics of sports were really just
envious of the public support and adulation received
by sports personalities. It must be admitted, I think,
that at least in some cases, this attitude on the part of
coaches, athletes, and sports fans has not been without
some justification.

A cursory look at the history of American sports re-
veals that, for the most part, the attacks on sports by
critics outside the sports world only served to heighten
group solidarity among sportsmen. For example, a college athlete who was treated as a "dumb jock" by the
faculty and his fellow students would find security and
comfort hanging around his college's athletic department regardless of how racist or dehumanizing the conditions in athletics were. His coaches may have treated
him roughly or even unfairly, but they never attacked
him for being what he saw himself to be—an athlete.
This point cannot be emphasized too much. With few
exceptions, a dedicated athlete in his late teens or early
twenties gets nearly his entire identity from his sports
involvement. Consequently, an attack on him as an
athlete, or even a criticism of sports in general, takes
on devastating dimensions. (Professors, like myself, who
have taught college courses that rigorously examine the
role of sports in American society have discovered this
phenomenon firsthand, whenever they have had athletes in their courses. I barely survived teaching such
a course at the University of California at Berkeley

where over a hundred of the four hundred students enrolled in the course were varsity athletes.)

The most intelligent, perceptive writing being done on American sports in the last ten years has come from journalists and athletes. The writings of David Wolf, Leonard Shecter, Bob Lipsyte, and Dave Meggyesy have contributed more to an intelligent analysis of American sports than the work of any ten American academics combined. I make this statement primarily to highlight the default of American physical educators and other scholars who claim sports as their area of study. In athletic terms, their work has been about as outstanding as a 4:25 mile at the national track and field championships.

Most American physical educators have been caught up in the mythology of sports as a character-building activity without which our society would be on the verge of collapse. They have ignored, either consciously or unconsciously, the reality of what was occurring right before their very eyes. (In scholarly terms, their work was value-laden and unscientific.) No serious studies ever substantiated their claims for sports, and the best evidence they could offer was testimonials from military generals about how varsity athletes make good soldiers. Much to their chagrin, this argument only played into the hands of sports critics who had been attempting for years to show that American sports was a militaristic, authoritarian activity. Physical educators, not known for their acumen, were serving as data gatherers for their own most severe critics!

Those few physical educators who have wanted to study competitive athletics in a serious, scholarly fashion have usually been excluded from the physical education profession or, if allowed in, have been intimidated by the athletic departments of their colleges or universities. I am not the only college professor who has had his employment canceled because an athletic department and its wealthy influential supporters among the alumni perceived our teaching and writing as threats to their hegemony. Given this reality, it is not surprising that the scholarly work being done by physical educators is usually on topics far removed from the realm of competitive sports. Physical educators would, of course, claim that their choice of topics is voluntary and dictated by personal preference. However, given the scarcity of scholarly inquiries into competitive sports, in face of the pervasive effect sports have on our society, I think the facts speak for themselves. And even when physical educators choose to study competitive sports, they rarely seem to tackle any issues of real significance.

Today, a new group of academics have begun studying sports. They call themselves sports sociologists, and they have offered essentially the same criticism of physical educators that I have. Most sports sociologists at this time are not really sociologists, however, but physical educators who have taken some courses in sociology departments during their graduate-school training. The two most prominent North American "sports sociologists-physical educators" are Gerald Kenyon and John Loy. In their edited book, *Sport, Culture, and Society*, which serves as a standard text for physical education courses on the sociology of sport, they discuss their orientation toward sport sociology:

> Sport sociology, as we view it, is a value-free social science. It is not an effort to influence public opinion or behavior, nor is it an attempt to find support for the "social development" objective of physical education, as described in the writings of Hetherington, Williams, Nash, Oberteuffer, and others. The sport sociologist is neither a spreader of gospel nor an evangelist for exercise. His function is not to shape attitudes and values but rather to describe and explain them.

While physical educators are value-laden and unscientific, today's American "sports sociologist-physical educators" claim to be value-free and scientific. And since most American physical educators have little knowledge of the history of social science, Loy and Kenyon and their school have been able to convince most physical educators that their particular approach to sociology is the only correct, scholarly, scientific approach. Any orientation that is not value-free is a social movement and not scientific or scholarly, according to them. Being decent, honorable men, they are not against social movements; they just want it perfectly clear that social scientists like themselves are not members of social movements.

Even today, at what is still the zenith of the value-free school, it is fair to say that this position is probably not held by the majority of active social scientists in the world. One would never know this, however, by listening to our "sports sociologist-physical educators."

The evolution of sports sociology today is in many ways a microcosm of the history of Western social science. And if our "sports sociologist-physical educators" were familiar with this history, they would probably not so blindly espouse a value-free orientation as the only legitimate approach to understanding the social relationships involved in sports activities.

The value-free orientation came to prominence in Western social science when social scientists were unable to reconcile, as Ernest Becker has pointed out, "science with the larger design of human life." By the latter half of the nineteenth century, much of Western social science had degenerated into social-welfarism. Theory had become separated from practice, practice from theory, and most social scientists had become social workers running around trying to patch up all of society's ills. Social scientists, just like most physical educators, had become "value-laden and unscientific."

The understandable though regrettable reaction to

this development was for social scientists to purge themselves of all values and attempt to build a value-free, scientific approach to social science. The method of the natural scientist was seen as the apotheosis of scientific endeavor, and it was this method that social scientists attempted to emulate. The social scientist was no longer an airy theorist bound up in ideology, but a hardheaded scientist every bit as legitimate and deserving of funding as a natural scientist. American social scientists, in particular, were eager to eliminate any socialistic influence on the development of American social science. Not too surprisingly, they were not so eager to prevent themselves from being contaminated by capitalism. (One need only look at the *sources* for funding given to American social scientists to substantiate this point.)

It should be clear, however, that the development of American social science that I have just described was not inevitable. As far back as 1886, certain social scientists saw the danger inherent in this development toward a value-free scientific orientation. John Eaton, a prominent social scientist of the time, spoke out in alarm at the changes occurring within the social-science movement: "Let the warning cry fill the air of scientific associations, from meeting to meeting, that SCIENCE IS OUR MEANS, NOT OUR END. . . ." But the warnings of Eaton and those who agreed with him were ignored. Instead of returning to the Enlightenment hope of science in the service of man, the pursuit of science as an end in itself came to be the dominant position in American social science. And it is this tradition with which most American "sports sociologist-physical educators" have come to identify.

Any serious social scientist must admit, however, that the value-free approach to social science has always had its critics both within and without the social-science movement. The most scholarly, insightful, and comprehensive criticism of the value-neutral school of which

I am aware is presented in the work of Ernest Becker, particularly in his book *The Structure of Evil—An Essay on the Unification of the Science of Man*. Additionally, it should go without saying that Marxist social scientists have never accepted the legitimacy of a value-neutral orientation.

Douglas Dowd, in an essay in Irving Louis Horowitz's edited book, *The New Sociology*, offers an important criticism of the value-neutral approach. "To be uncommitted," according to Dowd, and I would certainly agree with him, "is not to be neutral, but to be committed—consciously or not—to the status quo; it is, in [C. Wright] Mills's phrase, 'to celebrate the present.'"

In another essay in *The New Sociology*, Sidney Willhelm attacks the value-neutral position from a different perspective:

> Through his ideology of non-involvement in the social effects of scientific research, the scientist is simply trying to free himself from social responsibility. And in doing so he creates a situation that no democratic society can afford: the luxury of an unaccountable scientific aristocracy. The scientist seeks to thrust upon our society his view of complete and personal freedom through the gimmick of aristocratic insulation. His insistence upon ethical neutrality is merely a veneer for irresponsibility by a group that will amass untold power. Like any elite that finally "arrives," the scientist wishes to camouflage the true nature of his behavior through an ideological cloak of non-responsibility which, in reality, will eventually come to mean irresponsibility.

I have offered this brief historical sketch of the development of American social science and sports sociology in order to make clear the crucial importance of this book by Paul Hoch. *Rip Off the Big Game* just may be the most important book written on American sports. I do not make this claim on the basis of a naïve belief that Dr. Hoch's historical materialist analysis is the definitive analysis of American sports, or even because I believe such an analysis could necessarily provide a definitive statement.

What makes Dr. Hoch's book so important is that it is the first work that really attempts to explain the causes of the various ills plaguing American sports. Shecter, Parrish, Oliver, myself, and many other writers have painstakingly described these ills; Dr. Hoch has taken on the Herculean task of attempting to explain why these ills have come to be. This task is at least the equivalent of a distance runner setting out to run a mile in 3:50. I will leave it up to you to decide whether he has succeeded.

Still, the merit of this book does not hinge on whether or not Dr. Hoch was completely successful. As in sports, the crucial factor should not be only the outcome, but also how well one competes or struggles. Dr. Hoch has struggled most valiantly, and his book will help to provoke intelligent thinking about the nature of American sports and American society. Hopefully, no "sports sociologist-physical educator" who reads this book will ever again be tempted to write another nonsensical and spurious study alleging that sports participation prevents juvenile delinquency or helps social mobility. Or at least if sports sociologists want to continue doing such studies, they should be too embarrassed to claim value-neutrality. Value-neutrality in sports, as in any other area of society, is support of the status quo. The data show this, and all aspiring scientists must be willing to accept the evidence!

It seems to me that only someone who is naïve, or perhaps someone who is being heavily subsidized by our monopoly-capitalist system, would continue to insist on value-neutrality as the only scientific approach to social science. In my opinion, the nature of sports in American society can best be examined and elucidated by a scientific approach. However, in the words of John Eaton, it should be understood that science is our means, not our end. As Earle Zeigler, one of North America's most respected physical educators and the dean of the College of Physical Education at the University of Western Ontario, has so aptly stated: "Man must learn quickly to employ and direct science in the best possible way to serve humanity."

Sports fans, athletes, coaches, scholars and anyone else who wants to understand the role of sports in our society will find this book invaluable reading. The fact that the book is relevant to such a heterogeneous group is perhaps its highest compliment. It is a scholarly work written in a lively, passionate, highly readable style—a very rare occurrence at a time where the jargon and specialization of the various academic disciplines has reached such a point that sociologists of one particular specialization frequently cannot even discuss their work with other sociologists.

As someone who has spent the best part of his life involved in sports as an athlete, coach, sportswriter, and social scientist studying sports, I was happy to discover that this book is not an attack on sports. Dr. Hoch's point is that the problems in American sports today are a result of the social conditions concomitant with monopoly capitalism; he does not see these problems as an inevitable development of competitive sport.

Rip Off the Big Game is an attack on monopoly capitalism, not sports. (Dr. Hoch himself was a member of his high school championship football team and his college track team.) It attacks the rulers of American society and the barons of the American sports industry, not the American people or athletes. In fact, much of the book is a tribute to those athletes and sportswriters who have struggled so admirably to maintain humanistic values while living in a dehumanizing system.

Jack Scott, Chairman
Department of Physical Education
Oberlin College

Next to religion, baseball has furnished a greater impact on American life than any other institution—former President Herbert Hoover

Sports and Society

Two American Sprinters Give Black Power Salute at Mexico Olympics
Anti-Apartheid Demonstrators Break up South African Cricket Tour
Vice-President Denounces U.S.-Peking Ping-Pong

Thus, a few front-page headlines of recent years. Football "jocks" blockaded occupying students at the 1968 Columbia sit-in, British soccer "skinheads" bashed Pakistani immigrants all over England, and South African sportsmen soundly beat up on their hippie population. As the '70s begin, every U. S. sports event seems to be turning into a pro-war rally, complete with speeches from the Secretary of Defense at the baseball opener, Air Force jets flying overhead at football bowl games, moments of silence for "our boys in Vietnam," and everywhere the flag and the National Anthem.

But when you look at the sports pages these days, you could almost believe that nothing has changed. There they still complain about "mixing politics with sports," as though the two had ever been completely separate. Oh yes, you read the occasional gripe about the "spoil-sports" who are ruining all our good, clean All-American fun. But mostly everything seems to go on as before—Yanks bash Indians; American men best Russians; the North clashes with the South; and so on. You could almost believe we were all back in the '50s with kindly old President Ike there to throw out the first ball, and everyone knowing in his heart that the Yanks would always win because God was on our side. But in the late '60s and today, what with black athletes damning their white-supremacist coaches, anti-apartheid demonstrators appearing at tennis matches, peaceniks fighting jocks in the colleges, it seems the world is turning upside down. But why pick on sports? What has football to do with politics?

"We play our games," says former *Look* magazine sports editor Leonard Shecter, "or watch them contested, with the same tenacious ferocity with which we fight a war in Vietnam and with as little reason or sense. We are taught from the cradle that we have never lost a war and that winning is everything, tying is like kissing your sister and losing is nothing." (*The Jocks*, New York: Bobbs-Merrill, 1969, p. 4.)

In a recent speech to the Touchdown Club of Birmingham, Alabama, Vice-President Spiro Agnew remarked that "sports—all sports—is one of the few bits of glue that holds society together . . ." But whose conception of "society"? And where there is disagreement about which forces in this developing society should predominate, how much does present-day organized sports give support to one side of the argument rather than the other? The disagreement about the values sports are communicating was outlined by Homer D. Babbidge, president of the University of Connecticut:

> Our teams and our players, by and large, are the guys in the white hats—they keep their hair cut short,

they're clean, they're orderly, aware of the importance of law and order and discipline. The students
and others who come to watch us play are the people who respect tradition and institutional pride . . .

On the other hand, he later continued:

Competitive sport is, in the eyes of its youthful critics, a part and parcel of the establishment. And
without wanting to be an alarmist, let me say that
I think that if the current undergraduate mood per-
sists, intercollegiate athletics are going to be a target
of criticism, disruption and protest . . . a prime
target. (Speech to the National Association of Col-
legiate Athletic Directors, June 24, 1968.)

And he certainly wasn't wrong. Since this speech was
delivered there have been demonstrations, strikes or
boycotts by athletes at several hundred American colleges and universities. And the athletes in question have
been demonstrating, not against sports, but against the
establishment's misuse and distortion of our sports. It
is also worth recalling that the most publicized student
upheaval in the U.S. of the past five years—the 1968
Columbia uprising—was fought primarily over the issue
of whether $5 million should be poured into the con-
struction of a sports gymnasium to replace a neighborhood park.

Curt Flood, the former All-Star outfielder who has
been challenging the constitutionality of baseball's con-
tractual system in the federal courts, points out that
many of the oppressive characteristics of baseball are
"of a piece" with similar oppressiveness in American
society generally. In his book, The Way It Is (New
York: Trident, pp. 16, 17), he says, "The hypocrisies of
the baseball industry could not possibly have been sustained unless they were symptoms of a wider affliction.
Wherever I turned, I found fresh evidence that this
was so." He points out that when he challenged the

right of his team, the St. Louis Cardinals, to trade him like a piece of livestock, the team's owner, beer baron August A. Busch, Jr., "advised reporters that he could not fathom what was happening in our country. He declared that my recalcitrance was somehow related to the unrest on American campuses. He was absolutely right."

In his book *High For the Game* (New York: Morrow, 1971, p. 126), Chip Oliver recalled that when he shifted from pro football to the National Guard, and was getting disgusted with the war in Vietnam and the military in general, he could have gotten into serious trouble for some of the things he did. It didn't happen. He thinks his superiors preferred to look the other way rather than make pro football look bad. "In their minds," he adds, "pro football is America."

But is it? If it were true that organized sports in America is synonymous with the best in American life—with "Americanism" in fact—why call them into question? Is it valid to "mix politics with sports"? There are, in fact, those who contend that politics is *always* mixed in with sports. "To me," said football coach Jim Sweeney of Washington State University a couple of years ago, "football and athletics are a fortress that has held the wall against radical elements. I look for them to continue to play that same role." Few people would contend that this sort of role for organized sports is not political. What it amounts to is one set of forces in the international capitalist society centered in America—namely the power elite and their coaching allies—*using* sports as a device for "socializing," and generally repressing, the working people's movements in America and her allies and neo-colonies abroad. In the process, the sports themselves are necessarily distorted by the political role the dominant powers in American society have called on them to play. This book, then, is neither an attack on sports nor on America. It is, in fact, a *defense* of both, against their perversion by forces less interested in sport than in their own continued wealth and power.

H. W. Morton in his book, *Soviet Sport* (New York: Collier, 1963)—a book firmly rooted in the ideology of the Cold War—claims that Russian sports are being cynically used to solidify the rule and status of the Communist party heirarchy. In fact, it is not very difficult to apply the bulk of Morton's analysis of Russia to America. Not in the sense that the United States has any sort of directorate of political functionaries sitting atop the sports world deciding how to use athletics to brainwash the populace (though Britain and Canada have had major government commissions on making sports serve what they called national purposes, and Britain even has a Ministry of Sport) but in the more general sense that our team sports developed historically in the elite private schools of those who controlled Anglo-American society. That, further, the sports themselves were shaped to fit the ideological and socializing needs of this industrial aristocratic class that was establishing its power at home and abroad. And that through the power of wealth and the distortion of sport into a money-making business, this class—or power elite of American society—is still trying to make athletics serve its general political ends of maintaining the status quo of wealth at home and neo-colonial control abroad.

In his *Economic and Philosophical Manuscripts* Marx pointed out that, just as a starving man is hardly in a position to appreciate what makes any particular food a delicacy, so it is with play in a society of alienated work. Sports cannot attain their full stature in a society in which they are forced to play the role of a temporary escape or pleasant-change-of-pace from meaningless work; where they are constantly used to sell consumer goods, from ski pants in pastel colors to "manlier" beers to "sportscars with drive"; and where they are enrolled in the ideological service of militarism, war, and preparation for future war.

There is clearly a certain artistry in a well-played game of ball, in the smoothness with which the players move around the field, and the deftness with which they execute their moves. Moreover, they are likely to derive important physical and psychological benefits from the game, provided that the external incentives toward intense competition are not such that they completely swamp out the enjoyments of the game itself. Philosophers from Schiller to Marcuse have repeatedly pointed out the centrality of what they call the "play impulse" as a pathway to sensuous human enjoyment. What we are mainly concerned with here, though, is the manner in which this perfectly natural animal impulse toward play is so often subverted to transmit the ideologies and world view of the dominant elements in the increasingly anti-human society around us. Our quarrel is not with sports, but with the uses some of the most repressive forces in capitalist society would force them to serve. It is true, though, that some aspects of sports—and indeed some organized sports—are more easily used to serve such purposes than others. For example, escapism, consumerism, and elitism are more easily facilitated by the mass consumption of mass spectator sports through mass media than they could possibly be through more traditional forms of play in which everyone was a participant.

Similarly, some sports are far more adaptable to serving the cause of militarism than others. In sports such as football, rugby, boxing, or ice hockey (particularly in the "maim-or-be-maimed" form imposed upon them by the way sports owners use these games to make profits) the military aspect has no doubt become so strong that games are won, literally, by so battering the opponents as to *physically* defeat them. Injuries, bone-crunching hitting, and direct physical attack are not merely incidental here. In this society they have become the very essence. No doubt this is less true in such "non-contact" sports as basketball and baseball, although here too (particularly as the search for expanded profits leads to longer and longer seasons) the number of serious injuries accumulated in basketball is far from small, and the bone-crunching slide with cleats flying (particularly to prevent the double play) has become standard in baseball. Track-and-field is probably less conditioned by militarized elements than other sports mentioned, but here too the use of the Olympics as a kind of nationalism-in-a-jockstrap to promote everything from Austrian ski-ware to race-nationalism, the ubiquitousness of the pep pill, the emphasis on Manhood-with-a-capital-M, and so on, all show just how thoroughly this society has managed to impose its values on sports. If we are ever going to liberate our sports and our minds from these distortions, we have to understand the manner in which these games have been shaped, every step of the way, by the social system under which we live.

There is nothing natural or inevitable about the sports we play or the way we play them. Sports would be completely idiotic without a common acceptance of the rules of the game by the athletes and a common *social* appreciation of the game by large sections of the society. (This, in turn, is conditioned by the relation of sports to the developing political economy.) The sports most appreciated in a particular society, and the way in which they are played, in turn reflect the past and present development of that society; they are, in fact, a mirror reflection of the society. Thus, as the Vietnam war heated up, the more militaristic game of professional football rapidly surpassed baseball as America's favorite spectator sport. As blacks began demanding control over their communities, black athletes began demanding a greater say in sports. As women began demanding equal pay for equal work in industry, the cry was promptly taken up by women tennis players. As the class struggle heated up in the factories, professional athletes too came out in a series of strikes. Sports partake of all the main contradictions of society, including the most fundamental one—the struggle between those who have power and those who don't, between capital and labor.

In the case of football and its rapid rise to the top in popularity, John McMurtry, former corner linebacker for the Calgary Stampeders in Canada, has written that, "pro football is a sick society's projection of itself into public spectacle." He notes that the first principle of football is possession—maintaining control of the desired object (the ball) and excluding competitors by rule-governed violence from getting it: "Possession" the key to football, "private property" the key to this society; legalized violence the ultimate sanction of both. It is no accident. In football, as in competitive capitalist society, the aim is to accumulate assets—in society called capital, in football "points"—by outmaneuvering the opponent or forcing him (in football, yard by yard) off his territory. And in both "games" the end goal is more and more abstract value without upper limit or concern for the competitor. The status of the competitor is also comparable: In football, the truly professional attitude is simply not to think of him as a human being at all—he is a "position" to be removed as efficiently as possible in order to benefit the team's corporate enterprise of gaining points; the mask over his face and all the covering equipment reinforce his status of non-humanity. Similarly, in small-scale corporate life, business is business, and the competitors are just opposition to be removed or outbid as efficiently as possible. The most important building block of both football and business is authority, and it seems to be becoming more and more important in both every day. In both realms a more and more rigid and bureaucratized heirarchy is taking shape and trying to control more and more aspects of the workers lives, both on and off the field. "The one unforgivable sin of a player," says McMurtry, "is to question someone above him. If he does that, he's finished." The chain of command, in football as in business, moves from owners, who are virtually never seen, to managers and coaches, to the trusty vets, captains, and quarterbacks, down to the ordinary worker (or "player"). And not only is the heirarchy of authority getting longer, it is getting more demanding and all-encompassing. In football, like business but unlike almost any other game, every pattern of movement on the field is increasingly being brought under the control of a group of non-playing managerial technocrats who sit up in the stands (literally *above* the players) with their headphones and dictate offenses, defenses, special plays, substitutions and so forth to the players below. It is no longer a game. It's a business. And there is too much money at stake to leave this business to the players. If the trend continues, it will be a rare pro quarterback who will be allowed to decide on his own plays.

McMurtry adds that the authoritarian tendencies imported into the game are not confined to the field of play:

Football comes closer to political fascism, I think, in its cultivation of mass hysteria and its fawning idolization of the powerful. The correlation between the growing importance of political authoritarianism in North America and the increasing popularity of big-league football should not be overlooked. If this appears to be an accidental connection, consider such things as football players having the shortest hair and beating up protesters on college campuses; pro teams being sanctuaries of racism ("All niggers is chicken," as one teammate put it to me. "Some's just a little tougher'n others"); the U.S. President's favorite recreation being watching football; patriotic displays being most evident at football games; and dean of coaches Vince Lombardi's famous remark that: "We must regain respect for authority. We must learn to respect authority. A man must be part of a group and subject himself to that group. Discipline, this is what football is."

Exclusive possession, acquisitiveness, relentless violence, impersonality, ruthless competition, technological sophistication and strict authoritarianism—these are the dimensions of North America's favorite sport. Anyone who looks carefully at the society we live in, and who reminds himself that citizens and football fans are not different people, cannot avoid making connections. The game inside the stadium and the game outside are as alike as the adoring roars that greet touchdowns and police powers. (From a letter to the Toronto *Daily Star*, November 27, 1970.)

In the pages that follow we will explore at some length the relations between sports and the developing capitalist society in which they operate, the ways in which both players and fans are socialized for production and consumption, for their roles on the assembly line or in the Army, and, generally, to be docile citizens of a nationalistic, racist, male-dominated and militarized country. We speculate as well on what opposing trends in sports are developing as the official socialization process begins to break down. Nevertheless, nothing in what follows should be construed as an attack on sports. To "attack" sports would be like the old witch's attacking the mirror that showed her how ugly she is, for sports is nothing else but a mirror, a socializing agent, and an opiate of the society it serves. To "reform" the mirror while leaving the society untouched would change nothing at all. We will have humane, creative sports when we have built a humane and creative society—and not until then.

Needless to say, such is not the usual approach to the subject. Though hundreds and hundreds of sports books appear every year, virtually none of them take into account the political economy under which the athletes and fans are socialized and under which different sports have attained popularity. Some are so wrapped up in the game that such "extraneous" matters seem irrelevant. (Thus, *Sports Illustrated* published a book on the 1968 Mexican Olympics in which the only non-sports-sounding chapter was titled, "The Show Outside the Stadium." This turned out to be, not the student demonstrations during which thousands were arrested and hundreds murdered, but the world swim championships.) To many, sports is such an escape from reality that the political economy is too mundane to be mentioned in the same breath.

But sportsmen (and even sportswriters) can no more escape from their socioeconomic environment than they can live without the air they breathe. In fact, all of their interactions are profoundly shaped by this environment. By ignoring it, writers discard any possibility of actually understanding the place of sports in our society, and the ways in which involvement in sports—whether as players or spectators—affects the lives of everyday people. Instead, we are led to focus on the "superstar," or the top-notch coach, or whatever other successful All-American hero comes to mind. By some magic sleight of hand we are led to forget the tens of millions of others, on the fields or in the stands, who never become heroes but have their lives shaped by the game just the same.

If most sports books have any method at all, it is that of the gossip columnist. This is basically to focus on the fragment of reality at hand—in this case a sport —and dish up whatever inside dope, tips, or gossip may come to mind. Usually, we get some sports great himself, or his ghost writer, doling out a bubbling broth of his recollections to his hungry fans.

Clearly, this kind of book can never hope to explain the process whereby a tiny elite became the "players" and millions of others became "fans." It takes that process for granted, as something outside history, something that always was and always will be. Nor can it explain the changing character of play, or the changing popularity of different sports, in different social contexts, for it takes the political economy as outside the focus of the discussion.

In order to discover how a given social system can shape and influence the character of its sports, and how, in turn, these sports influence the development of that system and the people living under it, we need a method that brings the political economy right into the center stage of discussion. We can then discuss the development of the system's sports in relation to the development of the political economy itself in a thoroughly historical fashion.

We can, then, see how different sports, the sports industry, and the ideology of sports, arose as a consequence of the developing material conditions of capitalist society, and how the sports industry functioned to facilitate the smoothness of authoritarian capitalist class relations generally; how it helped socialize workers for their coglike roles on the assembly lines; how it built up a symbiotic relationship with the developing mass media industry; how sports and the media helped socialize workers to think of themselves mainly as passive consumers; how sports spread the poisons of competitiveness, elitism, sexism, nationalism, militarism, and racism—all of which have kept the international working class divided against itself; and, finally, how there has developed within the sports world itself a movement of athletes to build a more human society.

Such a historical materialist analysis of sports—and their role in this society—has very little in common with the usual methods of procedure adopted in almost all of our "serious" books, newspapers, television reports, and academic research. These methods tend to be both more *fragmented*—in the sense that they rarely try to grasp the interaction between sports and society in all its totality—and more *immaterial,* in the sense that they concentrate almost entirely on our *ideas* about sports and society, rather than on the developing political economy which necessarily shapes these ideas.

To begin with, the usual academic approach would be to parcel up the interaction of sports and society to conform to the interests and concerns of the various existing academic disciplines. Thus, a political scientist might concern himself with how our ideas about politics influence our ideas about sports, or vice versa. Or a Parsonian sociologist might ask what ideas in sports are "functional" to present society. Neither would concern himself very much with the facts that our present society developed out of something and is developing into something, that within our present society there are different ideas of who should run things and how they should be run, and that, further, these ideas are shaped in large part by who does and who doesn't have decisive control over the political economy. The very act of parceling the analysis of society, or the role of sports in society, out among the various disciplinarians—political scientists, sociologists, psychologists, historians, philosophers, ad infinitum—virtually entails that no total critique of the society, or its sports, can possibly emerge. At most our academics might come up with a few "abuses" here, a few calls for "reform" there. The criminology professor might duly come up with the discovery that law and order is breaking down on the playing fields, as in society generally. The sociology professor would discover that there is a "problem" with black athletes. The psychology professor would likely diagnose this as some form of anal eroticism, no doubt caused by weak black superegos. And similar mumbo jumbo. The literature is full of it. What this usually ends up in, then, is a whole host of different disciplinar-

ians—from philosophers to primitive anthropologists—
busily writing away about the effect of their little copy-
writed corner of reality on sports. And in each of these
little treatises, all other corners of reality are assumed
to be known and static, and none of them are placed
in any developing historical context. Thus, if John
Huizinga or Paul Weiss are writing about the philosophy of sports, they concentrate on the language or
general principles of games used by different societies,
at different times, under different conditions; and they
almost entirely ignore any effects these societal conditions *could* have had. We are left, then, with a "philosophy" of sports that stands outside history and outside
society, and hence is almost entirely worthless.

This way of explaining the two-way interaction between sports and society (or indeed between society
and any of its institutions) usually ends up in taking
the society for granted, as something placed outside
the bounds of discussion by parceling its aspects among
different disciplines. Each discipline, then, further in-
hibits a total picture of the interaction from emerging
by ignoring the results of ongoing research on the same
problem in other disciplines. Thus, our sociology professor who discovers a "problem" with black athletes
little imagines that this might have something to do
with the socioeconomic position of blacks in American
society, or of what automation is doing to the usual unskilled black jobs, or of the way in which the American
military machine dominates colored peoples around the
world. That's all outside his field.

The hope is that by somehow putting together the
insights of the various academic disciplines into how
their aspect of society affects sports, we can build up
some kind of unified understanding of the role of sports
in society. But this is impossible. When one aspect of a
system is varied—e.g., its philosophy—all other aspects,
from economics to history to sociology to politics, all
vary too. And to leave them to other disciplines, or in

effect assume them constant or outside the discussion leads to nonsense. The result is not a philosophy of sports, but a pseudo philosophy of sports *language*, derived under the false assumption that a people's philosophy is somehow independent of its history, economics, sociology, politics, or geography. In the final analysis, this "serious" approach of university academics leads to results not very different from gossip columns.

Perhaps the best example of the stilted irrelevancies of the academic approach is the book by Gerald Kenyon and John Loy, entitled *Sport, Culture and Society*. (Toronto: Macmillan, 1969.) It contains a whole series of apparently unrelated articles on sports in relation to everything from micro-social systems to Pueblo witchcraft. However, in relation to the place of sports in society's "social processes," the approach is supposedly to evaluate how well sports serves the existing social system when confronted with its "functional problems" of adaptation, attaining collective goals (imposed from the top), assuring continuity of beliefs and orientations, training, integrating, and co-ordinating. Kenyon and Loy conclude, "it follows that the social significance of sport might be profitably analyzed in terms of its contribution to the functional problems of society, especially to the problem of pattern maintenance and tension management [p. 86]." In their characteristic eagerness to manage the tensions of this society, our academic sociologists (who seem to regard themselves mainly as software counterinsurgents) completely lose sight of what kind of society this is: Does a small power elite dominate? Are masses of poor and black people oppressed? Do the existing (oppressive) patterns of this society *deserve* to be managed and maintained? No doubt such questions will be called inherently "unscientific" by academics like the disciples of Parsons. This book, however, will not seek to rationalize the status quo, but will attempt to deal with sports in relation to society both as it presently exists and as it might be in the future.

Thousands of people who don't know me
use my participation on a Sunday afternoon
as an excuse for non-action, as a fix to help
them escape their everyday problems and
our society's problems. The toll of providing that experience is beginning to register
on me.

New York Knickerbockers forward Bill
Bradley, May 28, 1971.

The world-wide enthusiasm for sports
events brings to mind the decadence of the
Roman Empire when similar physical ex-
ercizes formed a circus spectacle which
whipped up the tired nerves of paying spectators.

Alex Natan, *Sport and Society*, (London:
Bowes and Bowes, 1958).

2

Coliseums and Gladiators

A few years ago, on an otherwise quiet November afternoon, 6,000 citizens of Columbus, Ohio, poured out
onto the streets for what was to be perhaps the longest
and most violent demonstration that city had ever seen.
It lasted more than nine hours before it was halted by
rain. Traffic on the main street was stopped. Cars were
walked on, painted on, overturned. "Store windows
were broken," reported *The New Republic* (Dec. 7,
1968). "Police officers were manhandled by young
rioters; by-standers were hit by flying bottles and
bricks. And the mayor, who habitually responds to
peaceful protests by sending in his club-swinging D-
platoon, joined the festivities." Columbus newspaper
reporters, who had exploded with rage after long-haired

young people marched in Chicago, cheerfully reported
property damage and pronounced the whole affair de-
lightful. Police joyfully escorted the rioters about. And,
according to *The New Republic*, Governor Rhodes, who
had previously called out the National Guard at the
slightest provocation, felt it had been "a great day for
Ohio." It was a grand old riot. Clean-cut American
sports fans were celebrating football victory of Ohio
State over Michigan. The same thing happened in Pittsburgh when the 1971 Pirates won the World Series.

In the spring of 1970, with tear gas drifting in the
window as he wrote, the *Daily Cal*'s sports editor,
Lewis Leader, felt compelled to say something about
the Berkeley athletic department's use of sports to try
to convince everyone that things were normal. "People
are being gassed and clubbed," he wrote. "There have
been perhaps 50 arrests in two days. Dozens of people
have been injured. As I write this I can see police pushing a student into a window on the terrace. . . . Yet
the athletic department has decided to continue on
with its full schedule of athletic events." Similarly, he
added, when President Kennedy was assassinated, the
National Football League decided to go ahead with
their full schedule of games just two days later. Commissioner Rozelle's reasoning at the time was that the
country needed something in such a time of national
tragedy. A fix? Another weekly pep pill? And when
Martin Luther King was assassinated in 1968, Los Angeles Dodgers' owner, Walter O'Malley, insisted that
his team's scheduled league opener with the Philadelphia Phillies go ahead regardless. (The game was canceled only when the Phillies insisted as a team that
they would rather forfeit than play.) Leader concluded
his article by explaining to those sports fans who might
criticize him for not presenting "normal sports coverage" in the crisis that if we choose to adopt a business-
as-usual attitude toward crises by "pretending nothing

is wrong," then in effect "we work to perpetuate the problems."

Leader's comments have far broader significance than perhaps even he realized. Ours is, after all, a society in crisis. And in many ways organized spectator sports are constantly being used, with some success, as a smoke screen by all those who want us to believe that nothing is really wrong. Surveys have repeatedly shown that about one third of the newspaper-reading public reads only the sports news. What sort of a dream world are the sports editors creating for them? And with a year-round schedule of sports activity from football to basketball to hockey to baseball, packed with the bowl games, the world series, the basketball and hockey play-offs, it is extremely hard for many people to concentrate on the fact that we've been fighting a war in Vietnam for over ten years. After all, the war is over there, irregularly (and boringly) reported. Spectator sport is right here in every home town, consistently and colorfully reported, made immediate and exciting, made important. It is much easier to think about the "long bomb" that scored the winning touchdown than the one that killed fifty Vietnamese peasants.[1] It is much easier to get all worked up about the Big Game than about big unemployment, big grocery prices, and big military spending: "Were this excess energy not channeled in America's mania for sports, it might well be used in dangerously antisocial ways. The value of this safety valve function cannot be accurately estimated, but it may be of considerable social significance."

---

[1] Recent American administrations have been well aware of this, and in order to preserve an aura of "normalcy" during wartime, the military has collaborated in what amounts to mass "draft-dodging" by professional athletes: allowing them to enroll in the National Guard, rather than the regular Army, and handing out special weekend leaves so that the pro jocks won't miss the big games.

(Gelfand and Heath, *Modern Sportswriting* Ames, Iowa: Iowa St. U. Press, 1969.)

"I do not share in the common view that athletics as such is the curse of the American university," wrote former Columbia dean Jacques Barzun in 1954. "It is better than the dueling mania, the organized drunkenness, and the other *social and political substitutes current abroad.*" (*Teacher in America,* Garden City: Doubleday & Co., Inc., Anchor, 1954, p. 206, my italics.) "Sports and recreation," writes psychoanalyst Robert Moore in his book *Sports and Mental Health* (Springfield: C. C. Thomas, 1966, p. 74), "are particularly valuable as a means of partial outlet of aggressive and sexual impulses whether we are participant or observer." And Conrad Lorenz in his rather slick treatise *On Aggression* (New York: Bantam, 1966, p. 271) adds that, "the main function of sport today lies in the cathartic discharge of aggressive urge. . . ." If, unlike Conrad Lorenz, we do not choose to regard "aggression" as some innate quality outside society and outside history, we might ask whether there might indeed be serious shortcomings in our present social order that give rise to widespread frustration and aggression. And if we conclude that this is so, would we not have to re-examine the role of mass spectator sports in providing an "outlet" or "cathartic discharge" for this frustration, without in any way touching its societal causes?

Five generations ago Karl Marx called religion the opiate of the masses. Today that role has been taken over by sports. In 1967 there were more than 228,000,-000 paid admissions to major sports events, including 67.8 million at the race tracks, 35.9 million for football, 34.7 million for baseball and 22 million for basketball. Perhaps "opiate" seems too strong for all this. But what else can we call it when a country in the midst of a savage war that has left millions dead or wounded professes more concern over whether Muhammed Ali will defeat Joe Frazier than over the widening of the

Vietnam war into Laos? What else can you call it when
hundreds of thousands of Americans protest the war
by picketing the White House, only to find that millions more—including their President—are off watching
football games? What else can you call it when industrial workers are so rabidly involved with the fates of
their sports heroes that they are perfectly oblivious to
the exploitative conditions in their own factories?

In this connection it is useful to recall to what extent
our professional sports have traditionally been aimed
at potentially restless minority or disadvantaged groups,
whether as spectators or players. It is well known, for
example, that a disproportion of American football
players (and the first professional football fans) have
come from the coal and steel towns of Pennsylvania.
The same is true of English soccer and Canadian ice
hockey. These sports, too, grew up in the shadows of
the factories, and gave otherwise restless workers what
their managers considered "something constructive" to
do. American basketball has long been the sport of the
big-city ghettos, with the sizable proportion of the top
professional players now coming from the streets of
New York's Harlem ghetto. The same holds for American boxing and professional wrestling. These sports
have traditionally formed the spectator pastimes of
newly arrived immigrant groups and lately of the racially oppressed black and Latin population.

What we mean by an "opiate" is anything that tends
to frustrate the solution of social problems by providing
individuals with either (1) a temporary high (or as
Bill Bradley put it, a "fix") which takes their minds off
the problem for a while but does nothing to deal with
it; or (2) a distorted frame of reference or identification which encourages them to look for salvation
through patently false channels. Things like sports
spectacles, whiskey, and repressively desublimated sex
provide examples of opiates of the first kind. If we believe that the solution to the problems of monopoliza-

tion of wealth and power will come through working people getting together to build a more democratic and egalitarian world, then, clearly, things like nationalism, racism, and sexism provide opiate barriers of the second kind. In particular, these poisonous ideologies encourage workers to seek their salvation in their nation, race, or sex, and thus divide working people one from the other, even one *against* the other. Religion probably provides an example of an opiate in both senses. Church going, prayer, and hymn singing provide the temporary fixes. And Christian theology encourages people to look for salvation in the next world, even as their lives in this one go to hell.

These different opiates tend to reinforce one another. Sports, whiskey, and sexism come together in the cult of the hard-drinking, hard-loving, hard-fighting he-man. On the other hand, the Fellowship of Christian Athletes, an organization of around 20,000 coaches, athletes, and ordinary churchgoers, has been using clean-living sports heroes to sell religion. (In fact, today's team sports were originated in England in the last century by a movement led by such people as Thomas Hughes and Charles Kingsley, who were called the "muscular Christians" because they believed that sports was the best socializer for a Christian temperament.) We shall give a detailed discussion in later chapters of how sports acts as an important socializing agent for misdirected elitism, nationalism, racism, and sexism, thus tending to turn jocks into protofascists.

At a recent sports symposium held at Queens College, New York *Times* sportswriter Leonard Koppett remarked that if we are going to call sports the opiate of the people, we might as well say the same about all the other products of the mass media and all other forms of mass entertainment. Berkeley sociology professor Harry Edwards replied that, be that as it may, there is one thing that makes sports watching a more efficient opiate from the power elite's point of view than virtually any other—namely, the total sense of *identification* of the spectators with the values and personalities being communicated from the field. A man might watch a war movie on television, says Edwards, but he doesn't normally jump up and down in his seat, screaming, "kill the enemy," and cheering every time "his" army makes a breakthrough. But while watching a football game, he can be both drugged out of taking any action that might upset the present *status quo,* and also drugged in a most efficient way into accepting the values and world view of the present *status quo.*

A good example of the opiate-oriented pattern of thinking is the following "explanation" of why football has become America's most popular spectator sport. This argument was put forward by Dr. Ernest Dichter, head of the Institute of Motivational Research, one of America's top corporate consulting firms. Football's popularity, he says, can be explained by four factors. First, the illicit violence in today's society—riots, student uprisings, bombings, crime in the streets, and revolutionary deeds—are all frustrating to the (well-socialized) citizen because, says Dichter, they represent chaos without control and flaunting of law and rules. By contrast, the clean, hard violence of football is refreshing and reassuring, because it is done according to rules. The referee is obeyed. Lawbreakers are promptly penalized. And everything is "neatly and firmly controlled." This, then, is the *opiate* of officialized, rule-governed football violence (in which the referees and judges have the final say). This, in turn, provides powerful ideological support for the officialized, rule-governed violence in society, in which judges have the final say. In short, the fans are supposed to identify with the distorted framework of law and order, both on the football field and in society, irrespective of what that law and order is supposed to protect.

Dichter's second explanation for football watching is that it acts as an "encounter group" therapy. Even the television fan in his living room partakes in the strong in-group feeling of the spectator. He is a member of the fan group and, as a result, "his response to the progress of the game takes on an unconscious crowd behavior." If he actually attends the game, he can have an even more vivid encounter session with the other spectators, yelling at each other and at the players and patting each other on the back when "our" team scores, and in general purging his pent-up emotions. (Maybe even yelling, "Kill the ump"?) This is, in reality, a plug for various opiates—identification with the fan tribe (tribalism), identification with a team (team nationalism), or the temporary emotional purge or "fix." The demand for these opiates probably provides the most common explanation for the public rituals of mass-spectator sports watching. For example, wrestler "Whipper" Billy Watson once remarked that, for fans to watch live wrestling "is a good way to release their pent-up emotions. If they can't take it out on their boss, yelling for their favorite or giving the Bronx cheer to his opponent is good for them." But is this really so? Sports may be "good" for them (and particularly for their bosses) as a temporary fix, which enables them to function in an oppressive job environment, but it does nothing whatever to remove the causes of that oppression. In fact, it exhausts so much time, energy, conversation, and thought that it pretty well ensures that the real problems will never even be discussed, much less solved.

The third reason for football's popularity today, says Dichter, is that it provides a reassurance of masculinity in a society in which the ordinary male has fewer and fewer opportunities to "prove" he is a "man." By identifying with the he-men on the field, even just as a living-room TV watcher, the fan helps revive the drives of the strong, assertive male animal. Women, says our big business motivational researcher, should stay away at such times because men resent their horning in on this "male" activity. And to bolster this special right, men alone become the "experts," knowing all the ins and outs of every play, statistics, and fine points of the game.

This shows, as nothing else, how completely inane the celebration of masculinity has become. Instead of identifying with the people with whom he must solve his social problems or suffocate—including his own wife —the "fan" is supposed to identify with the beefsteaks on "his" team.[2] And just so he can conduct his own alienation in this way without women horning in, he memorizes reams of trivial fine points and statistics. Salvation supposedly lies in masculinity. And what a debased kind of masculinity. The kind measured in touchdowns.

The fourth high that sports fans can get out of football is a crutch for their Spartan ethic. Dichter calls it the congeniality of hard working, clean living, disciplined young men. This is supposedly of special importance to fans who see the younger generation as having gone soft and fat with affluence, populated with boys who look "like girls," and who would scoff at athletes as "tools" of professionalism. So the true football fan sees his heroes as respected, clean, fair-minded, team-spirited young men who typify the way they feel

[2] On September 19, 1971, the United Press reported that Eulalia Fuchs, a forty-four-year-old housewife, had been charged with the second-degree murder of her husband, following an argument over whether or not they would watch the Cincinnati Bengals-Philadelphia Eagles football game. She reportedly preferred to listen to the stereo. Chataway and Goodhart, in their book *War Without Weapons* (London: W. H. Allen, 1968), note that "Some wives apparently live in dread of Saturdays and wait apprehensively to see what mood their husbands will return home in after the football match. If the local side loses, a wife may fear her husband will return home the worse for drink and give her a thrashing to get rid of the anger he feels about the lost game." Apparently as an opiate for the other opiate?

men should live and behave. In other words, "Good Guys versus Bad Guys." The situation is almost reminiscent of a cops-and-robbers soap opera. Unfortunately, most American sports fans have the same Manichean "Good versus Evil" view of the world, with this country on the side of Good. Here the opiates leading to salvation include clean living (clean language, religion, and sexual repression), hard work (irrespective of who or what the work is for), and discipline (which usually means obedience).

N. and H. Howell have noted that "during the depression years participation in sports greatly increased. [Many] turned to sports to boost their morale during those dark years." (*Sports and Games in Canadian Life,* Toronto: Macmillan, 1969.) Of course this was no accident. Governments were willing to put a good deal of money into sports as a way of keeping the restless masses quiet. In America, they suddenly discovered the heretofore peripheral sport of basketball and started building courts everywhere. More recently, Congressman Emanuel Celler has said that, "Pro football provides the circus for the hordes." Avery Brundage, President of the International Olympic Committee, has reportedly stated that, as investment in sports facilities increases, the amount necessary for police, prisons, and hospitals decreases. This may seem straightforward enough to the Establishment, but if we see police, prisons, and mental hospitals as part of the state apparatus by which one class imposes its rule on another, then clearly the opiate of sports must be classified as part of the ideological police force by which one class keeps another in line.

If one is going to supply the harmless outlets for pent-up frustrations and vicarious violence of a Roman amphitheater, it is a good idea to have some gladitors around. In professional boxing this is straightforward

enough. And arranging the big shows so that each
gladiator has a clear-cut (and harmless) social significance for fans to identify with is not that difficult,
either. In a racist society, the main bouts are usually
between "Big Bad Niggers" and either "Great White
Hopes" or obvious "Uncle Toms." (In his day, Jack
Johnson met one Great White Hope after another and,
in our own, Muhammed Ali has been matched against
a long series of Uncle Toms.) Even in the gladiatorial
game of professional ice hockey—in which fighting is
an integral part of playing—the same verbiage is often
applied. A Toronto paper recently remarked that,
"Hadfield, a resolute left wing (for the New York
Rangers), would win any White Hope tournament that
did not contain John Ferguson." So, too, for the black
and white gladiators of professional football, with their
helmets and face masks reminiscent of their predeces-
sors of the Roman coliseum. The area between the two
lines is even called "the pit." A recent biography of
smashing pass-rusher Deacon Jones is called *Life in the
Pit*. It strikes me as odd that even as firm a supporter
of college football as Max Rafferty can casually call the
participants "gridiron gladiators." What does this say
about the society that encourages them to be gladiators? (It should also be pointed out that, as in Ancient
Rome, the professional "gladiators" are drawn primarily
from the lowest social classes—including especially the
most recently arrived immigrant groups and the largest
oppressed racial group.)

The level of violence today far surpasses anything
the Romans could offer. A recent article in the Toronto
Globe and Mail estimated that 50,000 knee operations
are being performed in the United States every year
as a result of football injuries. The yearly death toll
from the "game" runs around forty. "Any time you get
a chance to put that head gear on 'em," highly respected Texas University football coach Darell Royal
told his players before the 1971 Cotton Bowl game (his

instructions were later broadcast on national television by ABC), "any time you get a chance to take 'em out . . . I expect and I encourage you to do it." Or again, "We got a letter from Headquarters," begins one of the main cheers of the University of New Mexico Loboes football team. "What did 'e say? What did 'e say?" answers the crowd. Then everyone cheers, "He said, 'HIT TO KILL, BOYS!' "

An article in the Toronto *Star's Canadian Magazine* quoted NHL president Clarence Campbell as saying that the fist fight in hockey is an inevitable part of the sport: "fighting is the emotional outlet in a game that is prone to violence." And a Toronto *Star* review of Brian Connacher's book on the National Hockey League wondered whether hockey "has become a game of dim-witted gladiators—whether, in fact, the game is fated to go the way of bull-baiting, lion-feeding, and similar sanguinary spectacles."

A sociology professor writing an article on the criminology of sports in the British journal *The New Society* notes that law and order on the playing fields is breaking down. Joe Namath says, "The name of the game [in football] is kill the quarterback!" There are hatchet-men (often called "policemen") in every sport whose only job is to put the opposition's best player in the hospital.

These are not "natural" phenomena, but reflections of the increasing preoccupation with officialized and controlled violence in society generally, as well as the system's ability to encourage people to displace their pent-up frustrations into demands for sacrificial thrashings. And if the fans can be encouraged by their society to demand higher and higher levels of gladiatorial violence, sports owners can easily supply it. Professional athletes are encouraged to maim one another, not only by the macho-minded sportswriters and fans cheering them on from the side lines, but by the knowledge that if they're not tough enough there are literally thousands of minor league and college players around to take their jobs. It's the old reserve army of labor breathing down their necks, making the competition for jobs on pro teams one of the most murderous dog-eat-dog struggles since the Roman amphitheater. The players simply cannot let down. They have to be aggressive, have to give out one better than they get, have to protect their jobs. In a militarized society, gladiatorial combat brings in profits at the box office. So it's all part of the game. But whose game?

An article in a March 1972 issue of the *Sporting News* by long-time hockey writer Stan Fischler notes that ". . . violence remains part of the woof and warp of the game, mostly because the men who run big league hockey want it that way." Fischler goes on to quote Conn Smythe, who for many years managed the Toronto Maple Leafs and is regarded as one of the "pioneers" of the NHL, and who set the official attitude that still applies today when he declared, "Yes, we've got to stamp out this sort of thing or people are going to keep buying tickets." Fischler also quotes former Eastern Hockey League player George Forgie, who said that fights, "preferably with blood," are "what they tell us to give them." The latter gladiator even recalls one pregame fight between himself and Bob Taylor that resulted in both being called to the league commissioner's office. "You know what the commissioner did?" Forgie asks. "He gave us hell for fighting during warm-up before all the fans could get to their seats to enjoy it." This is the kind of gladiatorial combat that owners can make money from. And that keeps the fans "happy."

> Hunger is hunger; but the hunger that is satisfied with cooked meat eaten with fork and knife is a different kind of hunger from the one that devours raw meat with the aid of hands, nails, and teeth. Not only the object of consumption, but also the manner of consumption is created by production, not only objectively but also subjectively. Production thus creates the consumers.
>
> Marx

3

Child of Monopoly Capital

Play is play. It seems to exist in one form or another in all human societies and throughout much of the animal kingdom. But the character of what passes for "play" is decisively shaped by the social system in which it occurs; and so, too, are both the "players" and the nonplayers. Indeed, one may well wonder whether the production of sports spectacles—complete with socially shaped rules and regulations, stadiums, mass media coverage, advertising, and the strong overtones of a profit-making business—has all that much in common with the play of primitive peoples, or whether it is, in fact, something qualitatively different, something more readily understandable in the language of money and profit than in the myths of good, clean fun and games.

Not too many fans realize to what extent actual play on the sports field is conditioned by the business interests of the industry. The mere incidence of some of our most popular sports reflects their profitability to promoters. Thus, for example, in 1926 (in a period of substantial investment capital surplus and rising consumer buying power) the owners of boxing arenas in the larger American cities noticed that their property was being underutilized between fights and circuses, and in order to use their capital more intensively, they decided to bring in a league of Canadian hockey teams to keep arenas filled. Just after World War II, in a period of similar economic boom, the same arena owners decided they could fill their houses even more thoroughly by creating what was to become the National Basketball Association. So, ultimately, the fact that large numbers of Americans play basketball or ice hockey is partly a consequence of the fact that a tiny group of entrepreneurs had empty boxing arenas available. (Here a material condition of sports production— namely an arena—actually "creates" a sport, at least for the masses of people who otherwise would never have been tempted to play or watch it.) Similarly, the "sport" of auto racing was created largely by auto manufacturers to sell their cars, and more recently we have seen the producers of snowmobiles trying to create the sport of "ski-doo racing," the producers of scuba equipment trying to create "underwater hockey," and so on.

It might be argued that since ice hockey and basketball "existed" before there were major leagues in these sports, we may be confusing "pure" sport with sports promotion. In fact, however, it is impossible to separate the business aspect from the play on the court. For example, the rules of professional basketball were changed about fifty times in the first ten years of the NBA, so that owners would have a faster moving, more attractive package to sell to the fans. Such things as the elimination of the center jump during play, the no-more-than-three-seconds-in-the-key rule, the width of the key, and the twenty-four-second rule were con-cocted because a fast-moving game with a lot of driving down the key *sells* better. Similarly in football. Chip Oliver (op. cit.) points out that it is virtually standard for offensive linemen to illegally use their hands on al-most every pass play. This is the only way they can keep the defensive rushers out. "I'm sure somebody along the line said not to call all the holding penalties," he says, "because if they were called fewer touchdowns would be scored, and that's what the fans come to see." They are called, he says, only on particularly flagrant violations or when one team is ripping the other and the referees want to keep the score down (so that the los-ing team's fans will come back next week). The same thing happens in all other sports. In basketball, back in the days when Bob Pettit was burning up the league, in my opinion he used to walk on his turn-around jump shot virtually every time he took it. But the shot was big money in the bank to basketball's owners; so noth-ing was ever said. On the other hand there were com-plaints from other players that all you'd have to do was touch Pettit and the refs would call a foul. This was known as protecting the star. With Wilt Chamberlain it was the opposite. When he was dunking 40 points or more a game, and the whole thing was looking so robotized that the fans were beginning to lose interest, it sometimes seemed you could guard Wilt with a base-ball bat without the refs calling a foul. This is known as "equalizing" things. Many people believe that, in both professional basketball and football, when a team gets far behind the referees readjust the penalties to help make a good close game of it. In general, the rules of the game depend on what is profitable to the bosses.

On a deeper level, the incidence of modern sports was something created by the material conditions of modern monopoly capitalist society.

It is a historical fact that only in the last century have the activities we call sports occupied the time of any substantial portion of the population. For example, in the city states of ancient Greece or the kingdoms of medieval Christendom, the labor of the overwhelming majority of the population—slaves or serfs respectively —did not provide an economic surplus large enough for more than a small aristocratic elite to engage in the fabled olympiads and jousting tournaments of which we hear so much. The laboring class of the population was worked so brutally that it simply would not have had the time or energy to engage in sports activity. In fact, this situation of almost total monopolization of sports by the ruling class persisted until, in the last quarter of the nineteenth century, industry had produced a surplus sufficient to support large-scale sports involvement by wide masses of people. This huge expansion of industry also went hand in hand with the development of an American system of banks, insurance, and trust companies, which together performed the function of channeling the economic surplus represented by savings into new investment (including the investment necessary to spark a new sports industry). In their book *Monopoly Capital,* Baran and Sweezy note that, "The growth of monopolies may be dated from about 1870 and has been proceeding, though at an uneven pace, ever since."[1]

[1] The 1870s saw the consolidation by John D. Rockefeller of his Standard Oil empire. According to Ross Robertson's *History of the American Economy,* the 1880s witnessed the rise of monopolistic trust controlling the output in the sugar, whiskey, cotton, oil, linseed oil, lead, and tobacco industries. Robertson notes that between 1888 and 1905 (despite the passage of the Sherman Anti-Trust Act in 1890) 328 combines had been formed, of which 156 had a degree of monopolistic control in their industry. By 1904 roughly two fifths of the manufacturing capital in the United States was

But there could be no mass hysteria about sports matches in the 1870s because the material conditions necessary to produce it simply did not exist: There were no mammoth stadiums to hold big audiences (and people wouldn't have been interested anyway); no mass media to keep everyone "informed" about matches and ballyhoo the "stars"; and no big interests in sporting goods, gymnasiums, swimming pools, arenas, and, generally, in selling the sporting life.[2]

---

controlled by these three hundred-odd companies, and perhaps four fifths of all manufacturing industries were dominated by such firms. Starting in 1875, with the exception of three recession years, the cash value of American exports exceeded imports in every year. So, if we take into account this favorable balance of trade, the rapid growth of foreign investment and the gigantic expansion and concentration of American monopoly capital, we can trace in detail the rise of an investment surplus large enough to support a new sports industry.

Similarly in Canada and England. The rise of monopoly capital in England in the last part of the nineteenth century produced the sport of professional soccer, and in Canada gave rise to ice hockey on a wide scale.

[2] One of the first such interests to develop in the 1880s and 1890s was the monopoly over the manufacture of sporting goods established by A. G. Spalding & Bros., Inc. Spalding, a famous pitcher and promoter for the Chicago baseball club, went into the mass production of athletic goods in 1876 (the same year the National League was founded). In the mid-1880s he began a rapid process of absorbing his competitors beginning with the A. J. Reach Company in 1885, Wright & Ditson in 1892, along with Peck and Snyder and many other concerns. In 1887 his "official league" baseball was adopted by the National League, the Western League, the International League, the New England League, and various college groupings. Around the same time the *Spalding Guide* was being promoted as the leading authority on all sorts of playing rules, and various handbooks were included in the *Spalding Library of Athletic Sports,* in which Spalding's own wares were

The first pro teams played before no more than a few hundred of the local gentry, who not only did not take watching professional sports very seriously, but usually scorned it as mere trumped-up commercialism and not at all fit for a gentleman to engage in for money or in any way identify with. It wasn't long before a few sharp promoters began to realize that in order to lure more customers to the games, it was necessary, somehow, to involve the lower classes with the teams. An obvious way to do this was to develop a local team, with workers from local factories as players and with plenty of local advertising. A sort of local "nationalism" for the workers.

Interestingly, these first pro ball games drew a lot of their support from a spirit of class rebellion. The first pro team, the Cincinnati Redstockings, even had a kind of "workers' control," with the players deciding how to divide up profits. Team sports had always been a pastime in which only upper-class amateurs could afford to spend much time participating. But with the coming of professionalism, some of the local factory lads could become players, and ordinary working people could identify with them and feel some sort of stake in the game. Many of the first trade unions were even willing to sponsor or promote teams. Snobbish upper-class newspapers promptly sneered at anyone who would engage in sport for money and paraded the distinction between "gentlemen" (i.e., amateurs) and "players" (working-class professionals). For example, readers of the *Fortnightly Review* in September 1893 were told, "The quality of baseball attendance has undergone an absolute change. Now it is composed largely of the same class of men as those that play ball.

---

liberally advertised but those of his rivals viciously derided. Nevertheless, this standardization of rules and mass production of sports equipment was an important stimulus to the rise of participation in sports in the last decades of the century.

Formerly it attracted men of breeding." (The same top-down aristocratic view of the world is still with us in the periodic hassles about preserving "amateurism" in our college sports, even though this might mean that only the rich could afford to play them.) Naturally, this sort of snobbish drivel encouraged the feeling—particularly with English soccer and American baseball—that the local factory lads were *taking* sport away from the rich and giving it to the working people.

The class-conflict side of it was, for the most part, drowned in money. New owners (whose main interest in games was how much profit they could make from them) started coming in. Factory bosses were quite willing to sponsor teams as long as the atmosphere did not become too "political" (i.e., didn't have working-class politics), and as long as the players set a good example of the respectful, obedient way bosses thought everyone—especially factory workers—should act. It was not long before those owners with the most money to promote their teams and hire the "best" players started to dominate sports. So the class aspect started to evaporate from professional sports, and, for example, baseball became the *American* game (the game that supposedly united all classes and helped build "Americanism"). In England the working-class aspect of soccer was never entirely lost. It just became a mythology which club owners can make money on to this day.

Of course, back in those early days after the Civil War, selling local spirit (or even a National Way of Life) wasn't all that easy; and, when you came right down to it, not many trade unionists considered buying a ticket to the game very revolutionary. Then, too, there was very substantial competition from—of all quarters!—the amateurs. In fact, long before the pro teams had set themselves up in business, enterprising "amateur" promoters had been charging admission fees to their matches, and when head-on competition between players' and gentlemen's matches began, the amateurs were quick to package their product in all kinds of rhetoric about gentility, true sportsmanship, and snob appeal. The pros replied that, be that as it may, they had the "best" players. Not many people cared. Attendance languished. And professional sports finances were constantly on the knife-edge of disaster.

One factor that made a decisive difference was the tremendous coverage of sports by the press. About the same time the first sports leagues began, there developed (not by coincidence) the sort of mass-audience-oriented newspapers needed to sell mass-consumption products. A symbiosis between sports and the new media was quickly established in which sports became *the* decisive promotional device for selling popular newspapers, and newspapers were *the* decisive promotional device for selling sports spectacles. (This symbiotic relationship between sports and the media, now including radio and television, is a central feature of the political economy of both sports and the media to this day.)

The rise of sports and the mass media went hand in hand with the rise of advertising and mass consumption. Mass newspapers arose to sell the products of mass consumption generally, from beds to boxing exhibitions. Kobre, in his book *The Development of American Journalism* (Dubuque, Iowa: Brown, 1969), points out that the number of U. S. newspapers increased six-fold between 1870 and 1900 (from 387 to 2,326). Their combined circulations rose from 3.5 million to 15 million people. Advertising revenue jumped five and one-half fold from $16 million in 1870 to $95 million in 1900. "Publishers and editors," writes Kobre, recognized the mounting interest in the new sports industry, "and began to cater to it to win wide circulations." This, in turn, created further sports interest, in an ever-snowballing pattern. He adds that the new "sports news" developed toward the end of the century "and became a mainstay of the popular yellow journals."

One famous press lord was once asked why, since he only published "news stories" about the products of promoters who advertised in his paper, he didn't make the same requirement for sports news. He replied that, in effect, the sports pages were advertisements for his newspapers! With this kind of love affair going on, it wasn't long before "sports heroes" vied with royalty as a vehicle for selling newspapers, and incidentally provided the embryonic "fan" with a hero image to identify with and to compare with other aspiring sports heroes throughout many long years of attendance at the games. Before long many newspaper owners, or their leading advertisers, had their own money in sports teams, stadiums, promotions, or products (and hence a much more direct interest in seeing that it all got top coverage).

Connie Mack, one of baseball's principal founders and long-time owner of the Philadelphia team, declared in his autobiography *My Sixty-Six Years in Baseball*, "The sporting world was created and is being kept alive by the services extended by the press." Mack's statement here contains a useful insight. It is, nevertheless, a tremendous exaggeration. It would be far more accurate to maintain that sports and media hucksters were able to "create" a mass-consumption spectator-sports industry within the context of the socioeconomic conditions that came into being in the last third of the nineteenth century, that is to say, *within the period of the consolidation of monopoly capital*. As Thorstein Veblen pointed out in his *Theory of the Leisure Class* (New York: The Modern Library, 1934), as long as most workmen were engaged in crafts or agriculture, in which they produced whole products for the purpose of satisfying clear human needs, they

had no crying need of systematic diversion, in the

way of sports, cabals, sensational newspapers,
drunkenness, political campaigns, religious dissension
and the like. . . . Diversions and dissipation extraneous to their workday interests are not greatly
required to keep men in humor and out of nervous
disorders so long as their workday occupation continues to hold their curiosity and consequently their
interested attention.

The gradual consolidation of the mass-production
monopolies brought about a tremendous bureaucratization of industrial work, forced the old craft producers
out of business completely, destroyed the old agricul-
tural and craft communities, and created a large industrial proletariat (including the cheap labor brought
into the cities via mass immigration). Division of labor
within the new mass production monopolies brought
about the narrower and narrower division of productive work into less and less meaningful and creative activity. So in a situation in which workers were given
less scope for creativity and decision making in production, it was only to be expected that they should
seek (and be provided with) some sort of pseudo-
escape and pseudo-satisfaction and pseudo-community
in comsumption. Sports spectacles were in the vanguard
of the new consumption opiates. Participation sports for
the elite was gradually readapted into spectator consumption for what was to become "the masses": a sort
of opium for the people. From the point of view of the
ruling class, the sort of passive attitudes industrial workers learn in watching a baseball game serve as a useful
socializer for the deadened passivity necessary to function in a capitalist factory. Inasmuch as the rise of sports
took place during roughly the same period as the rise
of militant trade unions, factory owners, not surprisingly,
tried to do all they could to direct their workers' attention toward the more sporting—and, hence, safe—kinds
of activities. Soon industrial capitalists were putting

money into baseball teams, and newspapers began to look with favor on "good, clean sports" as a pleasant alternative to trade union militancy. The consumption of sports was thus both an outgrowth of and an important bulwark to the bureaucratized social relations that came to govern production.[3] The character and scale of sports today is the child of monopoly capitalism.

[3] John Rickards Betts in his essay "The Technological Revolution and the Rise of Sport, 1850–1900," says that Lewis Mumford (*Technics and Civilization*, New York, 1934, pp. 303–5) and Arnold Toynbee (*A Study of History*, London, 1934, Vol. IV, pp. 242–43) have stressed that, in Betts's words, "sport is a direct reaction against the mechanization, the division of labor, and the standardization of life in a machine civilization." (Kenyon and Loy, eds., op. cit., p. 165.) He adds though that "sport in nineteenth-century America was as much a product of industrialization as an antidote to it." The words "machine civilization" and "industrialization" are unfortunately very vague and mystifying. What we are really concerned with is a very specific (monopoly capitalist) organization of this process, which robs people of their power to make decisions and their creativity, and sets them in search of opiates in consumption and entertainment.

Around the simplicity which most of us
want out of sports has grown a monster, a
sprawling five-billion-dollar-a-year industry
which pretends to cater to our love of
games but instead has evolved into that
one great American institution: big business. Winning, losing, playing the game,
all count far less than counting the money.
Leonard Shecter, *The Jocks*

4

Who Owns Sports?

We have already noted that the first professional baseball team was "owned" by the players themselves, and
embodied a kind of players' control over when, where,
and how they should play, as well as how profits should
be shared. At the time, most other baseball players
also liked the idea of this arrangement. It took more
than a third of a century to convince most of them that
anyone else should "own" their labor or their contracts.
(The basketball players took even longer.) And even
in our enlightened era, many are still not convinced.

Prior to 1876, when the National League was formed,
professional baseball players often moved around between whichever teams would pay them the most
money, or they formed their own teams. But the cap-

italists who formed the new league had other ideas. They had the money for sports fields, promotion, and players' salaries, but they insisted that players sign contracts containing what was known as a "reserve clause," giving their "owners" the right to reserve their services, and exclude them from playing for other league teams. This infuriated the players, but since these owners seemed to be the only ones around able to borrow the money to bank roll such a large-scale operation (and since a good many players earned big money "fringe benefits" by fixing games) most grudgingly took their pay packets and played the game.

In 1882, however, the American Association was formed. Although the new league also had what the players called a "slave system"—whereby owners doled out amongst themselves monopolistic rights for contracting certain players—at least now players could choose between the two leagues. This meant owners had to compete for them. But this free competition lasted only one year. The owners of the two leagues finally decided among themselves that monopoly was best for all of them, and they agreed not to hire each others' players. So the players were right back where they started.

In 1884, just eight years after the National League was founded, its monopolistic ways of doing business were put to a stern test. Realtor Henry V. Lucas declared that the reserve rule "reserves all that is good for the owners." Since it was time to do something about the player's "bondage," he formed a new Union League. Naturally, the threat of free competition did not endear itself to the monopolists or their friends in the press. It was all-out war. But, as its finances plunged deeper and deeper into the red, the Union League collapsed after only one year. As part of the price of peace and profit, Lucas himself was admitted to the National League as owner of the St. Louis franchise. Monopoly was still intact.

The owners had a good thing going, until they started

pushing the players too hard. As the 1880s ended they
were trying to establish a sort of productivity scale for
players, whereby each man would be graded on his
playing from A to E, with salaries ranging in five grades
from $2,500 down to $1,500. In effect, this would have
taken away the player's right to negotiate his salary
with the only boss he was allowed to work for. Full-
scale rebellion broke out. Under the leadership of their
union, the National Brotherhood of Professional Players, the athletes set up their own league. The National
League was decimated. Even by paying huge salaries,
it could hold so few of its players that it had to fill almost every position with rookies. It became known as
the sand-lot league. The American Association found
itself in a similar position. The Players' League
promptly managed to attract more fans than either of
the old leagues. Not surprisingly, other capitalists, including those who owned the newspapers, did not like
the idea of workers deserting a business and setting up
their own. So the new league found it impossible to
raise money. It could not get bank loans. More often
than not, its games received no press coverage. What
news there was of the Players' League amounted to a
new scandal "uncovered" every week. (In his book
Baseball: The Early Years, Harold Seymour quotes a
newspaper account of a players' meeting; they are reported as dressed in fur-lined overcoats, patent-leather
shoes, silk hats, with $5,000 diamond stick-pins, gaudy
rings, gold-headed canes, and smoking expensive cigars.) Without financial backing from the banks, the
players found it hard to stand up to cutthroat competition. In a year this most popular of the three leagues,
comprised of almost all the top players, had folded. The
American Association (which used to refer to the NL as
"the rich man's league") went down shortly thereafter.
The players had been beaten back. The rule of monopoly continued.

   The situation in other sports had been a bit better.

High school and college sports, of which football was rapidly becoming the most popular, were for many years entirely under the control of the players themselves. Intramural and even intercollegiate games were simply organized by the students interested in such things, without much interest or interference from school administrations. For example, in his book *The Athletic Revolution* (New York: The Free Press, 1971, p. 161) Jack Scott notes that in the 1860s high school football matches between public and private schools became popular around Boston, and 1869 saw the first major American college football game, between Princeton and Rutgers. "American schools and colleges," he says, "followed the pattern of Oxford and Cambridge during the beginning years of interscholastic and intercollegiate competition, and the responsibility for organizing athletic programs remained in the hands of the undergraduates." It should be added, however, that these athletic activities developed for the most part at highly elite prep schools and universities where no one would have dreamed of ordering about and controlling the gentleman-players in the authoritarian manner that has become so common today.

In the 1880s, however, two things happened. First, college sports started spreading far beyond the elite colleges of the Ivy League and the Northeast to places, including especially the church-run schools like Notre Dame, which had no tradition of student-organized activities. More important, as the popularity of college football grew, the opportunity was seized to turn it into a big business. It was not long before the undergraduate sports programs were taken out of the hands of the undergraduates, and placed in the hands of a small elite clique of alumni, usually from the wealthiest families, who could be expected to exercise the same disproportionate influence on the college as a whole as they did on its sports program. In fact, in a very real sense the sports program *became* the college.

Frederick Rudolph, in his book *The American College and University* (New York: Vintage, 1962, p. 385) points out that in the 1890s at schools like Notre Dame sports became, in effect, the main agency for student recruitment. Even where this did not happen to such a great extent, college sports were to the outside world still the most visible—usually the *only* visible —part of college life, and functioned almost as a public relations program, helping to perpetuate the image of the well-rounded college man. "By 1900," says Rudolph, "the relationship between football and public relations had been firmly established and almost everywhere acknowledged as one of the sport's major justifications."

This mythical connection between the college sports program and the fiction of the "well-rounded college man" was particularly ironic, because the college sports programs came into vogue at precisely the same time as well-roundedness was being destroyed by the increasing demands for specialization. With the possible exception of the elite Ivy League schools, the college regimen became increasingly the factorylike one of greater fragmentation of disciplines, proliferating bureaucracies, and greater specialization. Instead of "well-rounded" men, the grads began increasingly to resemble mass-produced products. "Progressive" educators decided not to attack this proliferating specialization, but instead to add into the high school and college curricula a "liberal" sample of "extra-curricular" frills, including athletic teams and intramural programs, student governments, societies, and whatnot. Then the high schools and colleges could still produce the specialized robots required by the new mass-production monopolies and yet claim to be giving everyone a "well-rounded" education. It was precisely the solution that the factory owners themselves had opted for when they introduced factory sports programs to "broaden" the interests of their workers. High school and college sports were drafted to serve as the Emperor's clothes for an increasingly empty and dehumanizing style of education. They were good public relations, and brought in money, too.

Until the 1960s the money-making side of college sports was still important. College football at major schools could be depended upon to provide support for every other sport, and probably a good part of the academic program as well (either directly or through the contributions a winning team attracted from wealthy alumni). And the emphasis was mainly on "winning" almost as an end in itself. However, in the '60s, in the era of expensive athletic scholarships and slush funds, multiple-platoon teams, and declining student interest, football at a great many places was no longer even self-supporting, and had to be justified, to an increasing extent, as basically a public-relations expense.

In basketball there was much more flexibility. Not only was the sport not invented until around 1891, but it was to be dominated by player-controlled teams throughout most of its history. This came to a decisive end after World War II, when owners of sports arenas in the big cities decided there was big money to be made from professional basketball. So they formed their own league (soon to become the National Basketball Association). In competing with players' teams and non-league owners' teams, their one major advantage was control of the arenas (i.e., the means of sports production). They did not have to be so heavy-handed as to exclude the other teams entirely, although this sometimes happened.[1] All they had to do was raise the

[1] Similarly, in professional baseball, when there was talk of a New York team in the proposed Continental League in the early sixties, the Yankees let it be known that it would not be welcome to play in Yankee Stadium. The latter had been built in the '20s, because, when the Yanks' popularity

rental price of the arena to the point where almost no
one could afford it. (The arena owners, of course, could
afford it, since in booking their facilities for their own
teams, they were paying themselves!) Thereafter, pro
basketball, too, was monopolized and controlled by just
a handful of "owners."

So throughout the sports industry, as in every other
industry under capitalism, control is exercised, not by
the consumers (fans), nor by the producers (players),
but by the owners of capital. It is they who decide
whether or not to stage their spectacles and when,
where, and how to do so. Ownership gives them the
power to dictate the complete development or non-
development of the industry, the very life and working
conditions of those (players) whose labor they buy,
and the nature of the product they produce. And the
basis of their decisions is, first and foremost, personal
profit. In this, sports owners are just like other capitalists (although some of them may, incidentally, be big
sports fans on the side). However their loyalty to their
capital will always surpass their loyalty to the team. If
it did not they might quickly find themselves out of
business. And there is a lot of money involved.

Indeed, the first thing we notice about the sports industry is that it is very expensive to become an owner.
When the first professional baseball league was formed
in 1871 the entrance fee for a team was just ten dollars. Five years later, when the National League was
formed, the price of a franchise was just one hundred
dollars plus players' salaries. By the mid-1960s, CBS
had bought the New York Yankees for $15 million and
later the Vancouver Canucks hockey team was purchased for $6 million. At these prices a situation is rap-
idly being created in which only corporations of substantial size, or syndicates of their executives, can raise

---

began to rival that of the Giants, the Giant brass booted
them out of the Polo Grounds.

the capital to buy a team. Under these conditions, a professional sports operation becomes little more than a cog in a giant corporate empire (or syndicate of interlocking directorates) and is run in the same way as the rest of the enterprise. "There's not much need, really, to document football's place in the great American free-enterprise system," wrote a columnist in the Toronto *Telegram's Weekend Magazine.* "All pro sports are run as efficiently, cold-bloodedly and greedily as any other big business with a lust for a buck." As elsewhere in the "game" of capitalist big business, we find boards of directors dictating from the top to their production managers who dictate to supervisors (coaches) dictating to workers (players). And the latter have been reduced to little more than pawns in a giant corporate machine concerned much more with profit than "play."

It is instructive to gauge the size of the American sports business. Every year about 300,000,000 admission tickets are bought for major sports events. An average take of at least $6 a head for admissions, confectionary, and parking gives an estimate of gross revenues of around $1.8 billion. Adding in revenues derived from the sale of TV rights brings the total to around $2.5 billion. In addition, a 1959 report from the First Federal Reserve Bank of Philadelphia estimated that such direct participation sports as boating, swimming, fishing, bicycling, roller skating, bowling, hunting, baseball and softball, pool, golf, tennis and skiing involved at least 286 million Americans and resulted in expenditures (mainly for equipment and travel) of over $10 billion. (The present figure is about double that.) In 1966 the U. S. Department of Commerce estimated the country's annual recreational expenditure (including sports and related entertainment and travel) at around $30 billion. We must also include the billions annually invested in such facilities as stadiums, practice fields, arenas, field houses, sports ad-

vertising, media equipment to cover sports events, costs
of processing and distributing sports news ad infinitum.
Although there is considerable overlap in these various
figures, it seems apparent that total sports and sports-
related expenditures in the United States cannot be
less than around $25 billion annually. (And this says
nothing whatever about the tens of billions made off
products marketed via sports machismo.)

And it's not just the proceeds from the games, or the
advertising, that makes sports such a lucrative enterprise. A 1963 article in the *Financial Post* noted that
preparations for the Tokyo Olympics had sparked a re-
building job costing a tidy $1.5 billion (including a
$550-million rail line between Tokyo and Osaka,
twenty-three new arteries and eight expressways into
the city [mostly from the airport], nine miles of new
subway, additions to the Tokyo police force and an
$18-million television center capable of providing
round-the-world coverage.)

In preparation for the smaller 1968 Winter Olympics, Grenoble built a new city hall, post office,
hospital, police station, school, exhibition hall, airport,
railway station, cultural center, and various multi-lane
highways. All told, it came to a $200-million investment.
The *Financial Post* described it as "Grenoble's hopes
of becoming a leading European city, an international
convention center, a city trying to establish a reputation
as France's 'City of Tomorrow' or 'Atlantic City' . . ."
(Nancy Greene, who won a skiing gold medal at
Grenoble points out in her autobiography that, with
this kind of money at stake, it was necessary to appeal
to a gigantic audience to pay for it all: "The result inevitably is that the Olympic Games descend to the level
of spectacle and begin to resemble some kind of
circus.")

As I write this book the New York Yankees' bosses
are negotiating to get the city to rebuild Yankee
Stadium for them at a cost of around $30 million. The

Detroit Lions' and the Detroit Tigers' brass are reportedly dickering to have the taxpayers build them a new stadium (possibly two) at a cost variously estimated as running around $150 million. The Yankees, it will be remembered, are owned by CBS, a corporation worth billions of dollars. The Lions are owned by William Clay Ford, vice-president and part owner of the Ford Motor Company, and reportedly worth around $140 million. Multimillionaire John Fetzer, who owns the Tigers, also owns the "Tiger Network" of eight radio stations as well as various television interests. And these are the sports magnates the taxpayers are supposed to be subsidizing to the tune of hundreds of millions for their stadiums! Meanwhile the Detroit Board of Health has termed some sixty thousand of that city's houses as substandard or unfit for human habitation.

In hockey, it's been a similar story. Without a big enough arena it was implied that Vancouver could not get a National Hockey League franchise. So Canadian taxpayers were encouraged to build the $6-million Pacific Coliseum. The government in Ottawa and the British Columbia provincial treasury each put up $2 million. The city of Vancouver added $1¾ million, and the Pacific National Exhibition (which owns the Coliseum building) added the final quarter million. The Vancouver Canucks were 87 per cent American-owned. So, what you had was three levels of Canadian government forking out about $6 million so that American millionaires could sell a Canadian game to Canadians.

One reason an aspiring sports magnate is willing to pay millions of dollars for a team is that the possession of a league franchise puts him in a monopolistic position in marketing his product in a particular city and hiring the players who will produce the product. The toleration by the dominant elements in society of such monopolistic agreements in restraint of a free-player market, as the reserve and option clauses written into all major league contracts, reflects the usefulness of the sports industry in providing a profitable investment channel for their surplus capital, and even more importantly, for furthering the sort of competitive, work-hard, be-disciplined, produce-more, consume-more ideology our capitalists find so attractive. The laws governing sports, including especially the 1922 Supreme Court decision exempting baseball from the anti-trust laws, arise out of both the economics of this capitalist industry and the place of sports production, including ideological indoctrination, in this society generally. Thus, the sports industry provides a graphic illustration of how, when the economic situation in a major industry violates the laws of capitalist society (in this case, the anti-trust laws), the laws are re-interpreted to agree with the economic "realities" and not the other way around. The ready acceptance of monopolistic practices in the sports industry goes hand in hand with the more covert acceptance of such practices throughout industry generally.

Under monopoly capitalism, owners are allowed not only full control over markets and players, but also tremendous tax loopholes. Since they have always considered players as "property" it was only a matter of time before they started claiming the same sort of depreciation allowances as the oil industry. The way this "game" is played has been described by former Chicago White Sox owner Bill Veeck in his aptly titled book, *The Hustler's Handbook*. When buying a major league team, says Veeck, you can imagine that you are buying their whole operation—team plus franchise —or you can claim to be buying a franchise plus a series of players. In the first case, the players would be considered an "existing asset, which the previous ownership had already written off at the time of their original purchase" and you would not be eligible for any further tax write-offs to cover further depreciation. On the other hand, if you bought "the players from the old company before you liquidated, in distinct and separate transactions," they can be listed as an expense item. "It said so right in your books." You can then depreciate the cost of each player over a period ranging from about three to ten years, which you estimate to be his useful playing life. "If you expect to make a lot of money fast, you're better off being able to write them off as quickly as possible." If not, you choose the longer period.

The key is the amount of the purchase price of the team you assign to the players, and how much you claim as the cost of the franchise. In the early sixties, it was customary in baseball to estimate the worth of the franchise (i.e., the part that cannot be depreciated) as a mere $50,000. This left the new owners free to list around 98 per cent of the purchase price as an expense item—i.e., player costs—which they could then use for tax write-offs. (In fact, during baseball's expansion in the mid-sixties, there was no charge at all for the franchises; everything was supposedly being spent for tired, old, cast-off players.)

Veeck gives the example of the sale of the Milwaukee Braves just before they moved to Atlanta. After deducting the $50,000 franchise fee, the "cost of players" came to about $6 million. Depreciation over ten years would then give the new owners an annual tax write-off of about $600,000. Or, put slightly differently, they would pay *no taxes at all* on their first $600,000 of profit (and since the corporate tax runs about 50 per cent, they would be saving themselves around $300,000 a year for ten years, or $3 million). "If you want to be cynical, you might even say the Government was paying half of their purchase price for them."

You might think that the owners would still have to pay taxes on any profits above $600,000. Wrong again. They can spend them on new players, and then start depreciating them. After ten years they sell, and then

somebody else starts the tax-write-off game all over
again. It is important to see that they are not selling
just a franchise and a team: they are selling, says Veeck,
"the right to depreciate." This is the real reason the
price of a major league team has been increasing stead-
ily, since the more the price rises the larger the depreciation write-off becomes. But at these prices a situation is being created in which only corporations can
afford to bid. CBS and the Yankees is the obvious example, but the Montreal Expos, Los Angeles Angels,
Detroit Tigers, and St. Louis Cards were all bought on
behalf of substantial corporate empires (a whiskey company, various television and radio interests, and a brewery, respectively). "A corporation," says Veeck, "not
only has the money, *but it can use the depreciation
write-off on its total corporate profits even if the ball
club itself hasn't made enough profit to cover it.*" He
adds that, of the ten American League clubs in existence when he wrote his book, only two were not tied
in some way to established profit-making corporations
that could absorb either the operating losses or the
player depreciation and, happily, "pass 50 per cent of
the price on to the government." No wonder Veeck says
our national pastime is not baseball but "how to make
sure profits can be claimed as a capital gain rather
than as income."

And sports may be leading the way. An article in
the *Financial Post* headed

Tax Break for Mental Athletes?

notes that while there have been a lot of complaints
that sports have become big business, "it seems entirely
possible that big business may look more and more like
big league sport." What with sports teams being allowed to depreciate their athletes, "why shouldn't fledg-
ling firms in other industries be allowed to depreciate
their new mental athletes?" And, competition between
companies being what it is, the day might come when

one of them might have to pay $1 million to sign up a valuable computer whiz kid. "The company will certainly want to find a way to spread that cost over the estimated useful life of the asset." Apparently, "all that has to be done is to form a new 'team.'"

All this may not even be the biggest part of the business. A few years ago the McClellan Senate subcommittee on organized crime gave estimates ranging from $7 billion to $50 billion as the amount bet on football every year in America. Per capita, the mania may be even greater in England. There are also close connections between sports owners and the bookmakers. For example, in his book *They Call It a Game* (New York: Dial, 1971, p. 187) Bernie Parrish writes, "National Football League franchise owners have backgrounds as bookies, racetrack owners, high-rolling sports bettors, and even tote-machine manufacturers." (It is also quite common for sports or arena owners to be big shots in jockey clubs.) A good part of the billions of dollars put down every year in the name of "sports" of course goes right into the coffers of organized crime.

But this multi-billion-dollar connection between sport and crime is not the worst of the betting mania. Much more damaging are the sociopsychological effects that go hand in hand with betting. Several generations ago in his *Theory of the Leisure Class* Thorstein Veblen pointed out that this widespread gambling on sports acts to promote acausal and animistic thinking in society generally, and to keep much of the citizenry in a state of drugged inability even to think logically. For example, there are few sportsmen who are not in the habit of wearing some kind of charm or talisman to which some winning magic or another is attributed. And, similarly, many fans will go through certain ritualized gestures while watching a game, or are afraid to leave their seats, or whatever, for fear of "hoodooing" the contestants on which they may have laid a wager. Many feel that by backing one side in the contest they have some-

how strengthened it. Others attribute magical powers
to a team "mascot" or crossing themselves at particular
crucial moments or bringing along their rosary beads or
what have you. (Actually, the belief in a sort of super-
natural intervention in these contests dates from the
medieval "wager of battle" and "the ordeal" in which
the contestant staked his life on the outcome.) But
Veblen notes that ultimately the gambling propensity is
"of more ancient date than the predatory culture. It is
one form of the animistic apprehension of things" and
its outgrowth—the belief in a preternatural agency
which might intervene in human affairs such as in the
wager of battle where "the preternatural agent was conceived to act on request as umpire," and to shape the
outcome according to natural justice. He says that this
animism tends to lower industrial efficiency, probably
disastrously, by interfering with workers' ability to com-
prehend causal sequences. However, it also induces and
conserves "a certain habitual recognition of the relation
to a superior . . . , so stiffening the current sense of
status and allegiance" (i.e., the hierarchy of God,
coach, team, and bettor, each having less and less
power to shape the result). "Those modern representatives of the predacious barbarian temper that make up
the sporting element," he says, ". . . commonly attach
themselves to one of the naïvely and consistently an-
thropomorphic creeds [i.e., Christianity or Judaism,
rather than say Unitarianism, agnosticism, etc.] . . .
which act to conserve, if not to initiate, habits of mind
favorable to a regime of status . . . the predatory habit
of life." The point is that without stakes and competition, and the divinely ordained system of winners and
losers they imply, there could be no stable, divinely
sanctioned social-status system. Furthermore, the an-
thropomorphic cults, betting, and the predatory sporting temperament are good ways of keeping everyone
drugged with animism and preternaturalism, thus en-
suring that they will be no threat to the existing social

dictatorship. This is more or less a refinement of Marx's religion-is-the-opiate-of-the-masses argument. Veblen seems to be saying that religion, sports, and betting form an interpenetrating complex of three opiates working in tandem. The stakes are enormously high—the perpetuation of the present system. As with the rest of sports, there's also a lot of easy money in it. Who's getting it?

There has always been a fair bit of centralization in the ownership of teams and facilities in different sports. In hockey and basketball, for example, the big-city American teams have typically been controlled by the owners of the major arenas in each city. James Norris at one time owned the "rival" Detroit Red Wings, New York Rangers, and Chicago Black Hawks of the National Hockey League. He also owned the three pro basketball teams in those cities, and the arenas in those and other cities. For good measure, he controlled professional boxing through his International Boxing Club, which had its main exhibition headquarters at his Madison Square Garden. When the anti-trust laws belatedly caught up with him about a decade ago, he sold off the Rangers and the Red Wings (to his half-brother) and broke up his boxing empire.

His present successor as chairman of Madison Square Garden is Irving Mitchell Felt, who is also chairman of the New York Rangers, the New York Knickerbockers, Madison Square Garden Boxing, Holiday on Ice, Roosevelt Raceway, Cinema City, the HCA Food Corporation, and the huge Graham-Paige Corporation. In his spare time Felt has also been on the executive committee of the Hotel Corporation of America, and a director of Sonesta International Hotels, the Mayflower Hotel Corporation, Fred Fear and Company, Recipe Foods, H and B America Corporation, and Columbia Pictures. He is also national vice-president and a director of the Navy League, and a member of the

Wall Street, Bankers, Lotus, and Harmonie clubs.
James Norris' successor in Detroit is Bruce Norris, who,
in addition to owning the Red Wings, is president of
the Norris Cattle Company and Canadian-American
Agys. He is also a director of the famous West Indian
Sugar Company, Dominion Foundaries and Steel, the
Midland National Bank (Milwaukee) and Maple Leaf
Mills.

The successor in Chicago is Arthur Wirtz. In addition
to controlling the Black Hawks, he is director of the
Consolidated Broadcasting Company, Consolidated En-
terprises, Forman Realty Co., American Furniture Mart,
Rathjen Brothers (San Francisco), the First National
Bank of South Miami, and Chicago Stadium, Inc. (Recently Comiskey Park has been having trouble attracting fans from Chicago's all-white suburban areas. It
seems that the blacks in the surrounding ghetto have
been less than hospitable.)

Another big hockey baron is Jack Kent Cooke. He
owns the Los Angeles Kings, the Los Angeles Forum,
Cable TV (which broadcast the first Ali-Frazier fight),
and a big stake in the Washington Redskins (of which
he is vice-president). He has also owned the Los Angeles Lakers and the old Toronto baseball team in the
International League. He is also president of a radio
features company, an industrial crafts company, an investment company, and has heavy investments in publishing and newspapers as well.

Montreal's top hockey fan was until recently Cana-
dian Senator Hartland Molson, who in addition to own-
ing the Montreal Canadiens, the arena and the Molson
Brewery, served as vice-president and director of the
Bank of Montreal, is a director of Canadian Industries,
Ltd., the Sun Life Assurance Company of Canada,
Canadian Corporate Management, Jamaica Public
Service, Ltd., and Stone & Webster (Can.), Ltd. His
successor as owner is Sam Bronfman, who also owns

the Montreal Expos baseball team, and is chairman of
Seagrams whiskey.

In Toronto, the men most interested in hockey were,
until recently, John Bassett, who is chairman of Maple
Leaf Gardens, and Conn and Stafford Smythe who
owned the team. Bassett doubles as publisher of the recently defunct Toronto *Telegram,* and is chairman of
CFTO television and the Toronto Argonauts Canadian
Football League club. Conn Smythe is the owner and
operator of Racing & Breeding Stables, a director of the
Jockey Club in Ontario, and president of C. Smythe
Sands, Ltd. Stafford Smythe is president and managing
director of Maple Leaf Gardens, president of a truck-
ing firm, chairman of Viceroy Manufacturing, a director
of Commonwealth Savings and Loan, and of C. Smythe
Sands. (In 1970 Stafford Smythe was accused by the
Canadian government of having evaded tax payment on
some $289,000 between 1965 and 1968. In June of
1971 he was arrested with another Maple Leaf Gardens
director, Harold Ballard, and jointly charged with the
theft of $146,000 in cash and securities from the Gar-
dens between 1964 and 1969. He was also charged
with defrauding the arena of $249,000 in the same
period.) Two weeks before his trial he suddenly died.
Ballard succeeded Bassett as Maple Leaf Gardens boss,
and, as this book went to press, his trial was still in
progress.

Typically, the hockey owners are multimillionaires
who own other large corporations, have close links in
the media and banking businesses, own the arenas they
play in, and also have big interests in other sports
(basketball and boxing in New York, baseball in Chicago and Oakland, football and racing in Toronto, and
so on).

In the case of baseball, the Yankees are, as we have
seen, owned by CBS. The Los Angeles Angels and the
Detroit Tigers are owned by Gene Autry and John
Fetzer, both of whom have close television connections

with CBS. Autry owns television stations KOOL in Phoenix and KOLD in Tucson, as well as radio stations in Hollywood, San Francisco, Seattle, and Portland. He is also president of Challenge Records and Flying A Productions. Fetzer is president of his own broadcasting company, TV company, music company, the Cornhusker Television Corporation, Wolverine Cablevision, and Amalgamated Properties. He is also a director of the American National Bank and Trust Company of Michigan.

Chicago's biggest baseball baron, at the time of writing this, is Art Allyn, the chairman of a major investment company, an oil survey company, a precision tool company, and Mono Containers. He is also president of Artnell Exploration, Ltd., a trustee of the National College of Education, director of Francis I Dupont, Hart Carter Corporation, Appleton Coated Paper, Vantress Farms, and the Allyn Foundation. His clubs are Executives, Economics (Chicago) and Mid-America. In Boston the Red Sox big man is Tom Yawkey, whose biography lists "management and control of mines, mineral interests, timber lands, lumber and paper mills in various states and Canada." Oakland's Charles O. Finley doubles as owner of the Seals hockey team and has his own big insurance brokers firm in Chicago. Cleveland's recent president Gabe Paul doubled as a director of the South Ohio Bank in Cincinnati. The new prospective owner, Nick Mileti, also owns the Cleveland Cavaliers of the NBA, the Cleveland Barons of the AHL, and the Cleveland arena. Jerry Hoffberger of the Baltimore Orioles is chairman of the National Brewing Company in Baltimore, Divex, Inc., and the Laco Corporation. He is on the executive committee of Baltimore Trotting Races, Inc., and of the Fairchild Hiller Corporation, and is also a director of a bank, a mortgage company, and a real estate holding company. The pattern, then, with the exception of CBS, is ownership by middle-range millionaires, with close connections in finance and media.

It is more or less the same in all other professional sports, though occasionally we find sports teams under the control of some of the "big boys"—men like Texas oilmen Lamar Hunt (who owns the Kansas City Chiefs and World Championship Tennis); Clint Murchison (who owns the Dallas Cowboys); Bud Adams (the Houston Oilers); and John Mecom, Jr. (the New Orleans Saints); as well as the previously mentioned William Clay Ford. The interlocking directorates of sports and the mass media are hardly surprising. One sells the other. They form part of a single complex. As for the connections with finance, it would be hard to find any big business these days without them.

Of course the claims of sports barons to their own feudalistic fiefdoms have never been entirely accepted. Other owners have repeatedly tried to cut in on them. And players, whether as individuals or through their associations, have continued the struggle as well. In 1901 the baseball brass of the National League were challenged by the founding of the rival American League. For two years there was a little free competition, but thereafter the two sets of owners agreed that there was more in it for them if they just respected one another's monopolies and exploited the players and fans together. In 1914 the Federal League was formed and promptly sued to have the whole monopolistic structure of the old leagues invalidated on the ground that it violated the anti-trust laws. The old owners were scared. But they managed to tie up the suit in the courts for over two years. Finally, in 1916, with the new league in debt to the tune of about $10 million, it was forced to accept a settlement. The Baltimore team was still unsatisfied and pressed on with the suit in the federal courts. It claimed, among other things, that the established leagues' coercive player regulations—in effect threatening blacklisting and banishment

for any player who associated himself with the new
league—had made it extremely difficult for the new
clubs to secure trained players, and this was a violation
in restraint of trade of the Sherman Anti-Trust Act. A
lower court agreed and awarded the Federal League
club treble damages of $240,000. A big lobbying and
press campaign on behalf of the old leagues followed,
and in 1922 the Supreme Court overruled the lower
court and gave the established baseball owners their
famous exemption from the anti-trust laws on the
grounds that the "sports" is not engaged in interstate
commerce.

In 1946 a good many of baseball's non-commercial
players were offered higher salaries in the Mexican
League, and they headed off south of the border. Baseball commissioner A. B. Chandler promptly announced
that any player who "deserted" to Mexico would be
banned from the major leagues for five years. A player
named Gardella returned before the end of the ban,
and was refused reinstatement. He took his case to the
courts, claiming that organized baseball was run as an
illegal monopoly that was depriving him of his liveli-
hood. The Circuit Court of Appeals agreed. Furthermore, Judge Jerome N. Frank noted of baseball's
reserve system, "If the players are regarded as quasi-
peons, it is of no moment that they are well paid. Only
the totalitarian-minded will believe that high pay ex-
cuses virtual slavery." (Actually, considering the years
and years of training, and the fact that an average
major league lifetime is about five years in baseball and
only three years in football, the pay is certainly not ex-
cessive.) Gardella won a handsome settlement. Much
more serious, from the viewpoint of all sports brass, the
case cast strong doubts on their continued exemption
from the anti-trust laws. Senator E. C. Johnson (then
president of the Western League) and Congressman
A. S. Herlong (a former president of the Florida State
League) sponsored bills in Congress that would have

granted anti-trust exemptions to all professional sports.
But the lobbying was a bit too heavy-handed, and the
bills ended up buried in committee.

In 1953, in the case of the United States versus
National Football League, the Supreme Court handed
down a decision that seemed to show that it regarded
pro football as *not* being exempt from the anti-trust
laws. The government had pressed for an injunction
against the NFL's practice of blacking out telecasts of
NFL games within a 75-mile radius. The effect of this
practice, it was stated, was to preserve a geographic
monopoly over all aspects of pro football for each home
club on its home territory. The NFL had opposed the
suit on the grounds that it, supposedly like baseball,
was not engaged in trade or commerce. The Court replied, "It is immaterial whether professional football by
itself is commerce or interstate commerce . . . radio
and television [coverage of games] clearly are in interstate commerce." The Court granted an injunction
against various NFL practices found to be unreasonable
restraints of trade, but not against the TV black-outs
themselves.

Shortly thereafter the St. Louis Cardinals were purchased by beer baron A. A. Busch, Jr., owner of the
Anheuser-Busch Brewery, and a new anti-trust furor
broke out in Congress. Inasmuch as the Cardinals were
a wholly-owned subsidiary of the brewery, it was
alleged that Busch was using baseball as an advertising
vehicle for his beer. Senator E. C. Johnson demanded
passage of a bill that would have made clubs owned
by beer and whiskey interests subject to the anti-trust
laws. (He claimed that in the past Colonel Jacob
Ruppert, who had owned the Yankees, had at least
kept the club separate from the Ruppert Brewery.)
What the argument boiled down to was the fear on
Johnson's part that unless baseball was kept separate
from obviously commercial interests, it would be impossible to claim it was not commercial and the game

would necessarily lose its anti-trust exemption. (Here he underestimated monopoly capital's ability to reconcile itself to violations of the law when there are big profits at stake. The Cardinals' take-over proved to be one of the first of a long series of take-overs of sports clubs by commercial interests, culminating with the take-over of the Yankees by CBS.) When the Justice Department opposed Johnson's bill as discriminatory toward alcohol interests, he offered to broaden it to include all commercial interests. The head of the Justice Department's Anti-Trust Division, Judge Stanley N. Barnes, stated that all of organized baseball, not just those clubs owned by businesses, should be made subject to the anti-trust laws. Under heavy lobbying, and a press barrage claiming that this would "ruin" baseball, the furor was allowed to die down, and nothing was done.

In 1955 the Supreme Court ruled that boxing was not exempt from the anti-trust laws, apparently because it derived approximately 25 per cent of its revenues from radio and television telecasts which are clearly interstate commerce. (By now both baseball and football were also deriving huge chunks of revenue from radio and TV.) Judge Felix Frankfurter seemed to be aware of the contradictory treatment his colleagues were giving baseball and boxing when he noted, "It would baffle the subtlest ingenuity to find a single differentiating factor between other sporting exhibitions . . . and baseball." In 1957 the Supreme Court again declared that the business of professional football was subject to the anti-trust laws. It ruled for the plaintiff in a case brought by Bill Radovich, a former pro footballer who charged the National Football League with monopolistic practices including coercive player restrictions and blacklisting.

Prior to the 1960s baseball owners had always opposed expansion. (After all, why cut up the cake more ways?) However, when Branch Rickey began to gather support to form a new Continental League, the old owners moved some clubs to the West Coast and quickly doled out new franchises in order to pre-empt the market. Around this time Senator Kefauver had a bill pending to bring baseball under the anti-trust laws, but under heavy lobbying from the owners, the whole thing was pigeonholed. The bill favored by the owners was one drawn up by Senator Philip Hart of Michigan (who is married to one of the daughters of William O. Briggs, the late owner of the Detroit Tigers). This bill would nominally have put all professional sports under the anti-trust laws, but it also would have exempted all rules pertaining to player contracts and territorial rights. In short, pro sports were to be exempted from the anti-trust laws by the very bill that purported to control them. For a while it seemed that they would get away with it. In August 1964 the bill seemed certain to pass. It was at this point that CBS purchased the Yankees, and a new furor broke out over whether a station that was dealing with a team for its broadcast rights could also own the team (though this situation had existed with other teams long before that and has, in fact, become common of late). The Hart bill was then sent back to committee "for further study," and has not been heard of since (though the senator from Michigan is still scrambling about after a substitute).

In the late '60s, players in almost all major sports began to band together in real associations (in contrast to the "sweetheart" associations of earlier periods), and began to attack the monopolistic reserve and option clauses. The best-known case was probably that of St. Louis Cardinals outfielder Curt Flood. At the end of the 1969 season the Cards shipped him to the Phillies. Trades are common, and provisions are made for them in contracts. If the owners "own" a player, they can trade him off, fire him, or ship him off to the minors. This time, however, Flood said NO. He wrote to base-ball's commissioner Bowie Kuhn to tell him that, as a

human being, he could not accept being traded like
cattle, without any say in the matter. He asked Kuhn
to declare him a free agent with the option of selling his
services to whatever team he chose. Kuhn conceded
that Flood was a human being, but not much more. He
refused the request. So Flood filed suit against the baseball owners, charging them with violation of ballplayers' constitutional rights and of the anti-trust laws. He
secured Arthur Goldberg as his lawyer and won the
backing of the Major League Players' Association. But
he had to sit out the 1970 season to avoid prejudicing
his case. In August 1970, a lower court judge ruled
against Flood on the grounds that "unless and until the
Supreme Court or Congress" nullifies baseball's anti-
trust exemption, "we have no basis for proceeding to
the underlying question of whether baseball's reserve
system would or would not be deemed reasonable if it
were in fact subject to anti-trust legislation." The decision seemed to be an invitation to Flood and the other
ballplayers to take the case to the Supreme Court, and
they announced that they would do exactly that. In
the meantime Flood wrote a very unusual baseball book
called *The Way It Is*, documenting the mispractices of
baseball's reigning establishment. Washington Sena-
tors owner, Bob Short, who seems to have made a
career of signing on good players whom other owners
consider too uppity, was able to coax Flood back for
the start of the 1971 season. But the long lay-off, the
sharp barbs of rival coaches, and establishment sportswriters, as well as unspecified personal troubles, had all
taken their toll. With everything closing in on him,
Curt Flood suddenly ducked off to Spain. Baseball's
owners were not sorry to see him go. But his suit remained to be decided. He eventually lost it. The Supreme Court ruled that any change in baseball's anti-
trust status would have to be made by Congress
(though Congress never gave baseball an anti-trust exemption in the first place). The Justices again empha-

sized that the other sports—excluding baseball—are *not* exempt from the anti-trust laws.

In hockey, the NHL's reserve clause[2] came under fairly weak attack from the Canadian government's Task Force on Sports. The Task Force members thought the reserve clause too unreasonable in terms, and suggested it would look less messy if it were replaced by the same sort of option clause that appears in pro football contracts (i.e., theoretically giving players the right to become free agents if they play out their options for one year at slightly reduced salaries). "An employer, of course," said the Task Force, "should have the right to restrict his employee from performing for anybody other than himself, but such restrictions should be reasonable in terms." Evidently, what was being recommended was "reasonable" slavery.

Football's option clause, a model in Canada, was being blasted by American players who had to adhere to it. "It doesn't work," charged former All-NFL defensive back Johnny Sample (after coming out of a hearing of a federal grand jury investigating pro football), because the owners "have an agreement among themselves" and enjoy "complete strangulation over the players." Sample also talked about the "blackballing" that forced him out of the (then) National Football League in 1966, and about racial quotas which he said are used to limit the number of blacks on any given team.

Jim Bouton and Bernie Parrish have pointed out that there is a National Football League rule whereby whenever a player who has played out his option is signed by another club, it must give full value for him. This amounts to a trade. If the new club refuses, Article XII, Section 12.1 (H) of the NFL Constitution provides, "the Commissioner may name and then award

[2] "The player hereby undertakes that he will at the request of the club enter into a contract for the following playing season on the same terms and conditions as this contract, save as to salary . . ."

to the former club one or more players from the Active, Reserve, or Selection List (including future selection choices) of the acquiring club as the Commissioner in his sole discretion deems fair and equitable." It is obvious that no team is going to give a substantial pay increase to such a "free agent" who has played out his option if they also have to pay for him with players. Here, too, the vaunted option has been short-circuited by monopoly.

Meanwhile, one of the Canadian Football League's own star players was having troubles with the option clause. Vic Washington, the Ottawa halfback who had been voted the outstanding player of the 1968 Canadian pro championship game, tried to switch to the San Francisco Forty-Niners of the National Football League without playing out an option year. He failed. The Canadian Football League refused to waive him out of the league, and, as the CFL and the NFL frown on "raiding" (i.e., free competition) across the border, Washington was left in limbo. Ottawa suspended him, and then shipped his contract to British Columbia "for future considerations." "Football," said Vic Washington, "just wants to make an example of me." (He is now with San Francisco.)

Basketball player Spencer Haywood did considerably better. Signed after his sophomore year in college by the Denver Rockets of the American Basketball Association ("The school is making a lot of money out of me, so why shouldn't I be making some," he said at the time), Haywood later "jumped" to the Seattle Sonics of the NBA. The Denver ownership brought suit against Haywood, the Sonics, and All-Pro Management, seeking to prove that he was still "Denver property." Meanwhile, the NBA sought to bar Haywood from playing in their league because their rules (i.e., their deal with the colleges) do not permit collegians to be signed until after their class has graduated. (This rule avoids the necessity of paying college stars big money to jump to the pros a year or two early, and for the NCAA it avoids the need to pay the athletes competitive wages while they are still being educated.) Haywood promptly initiated suit against the NBA, challenging, among other things, their draft laws for manipulating college players. The situation was clearly becoming dangerous for the monopolists. The NBA went to court and won a temporary order blocking Haywood from playing in their league. But this was overruled by U. S. District Court Judge Warren J. Ferguson, who ruled that Haywood could play for the Sonics through the 1971 season, pending the Court's decision on the Rockets' case. The Judge further added that professional athletes "cannot be used and cannot be treated as merchandise." This must have come as quite a shock to all sports magnates. Within two weeks of the Judge's provisional decision the NBA had come to a settlement with Haywood and Seattle. The league would interpose no further objection to Haywood playing on the Seattle club. In return Haywood would drop his suit against the NBA, and the club would pay the NBA $200,000 in fines for violating the league by-laws. At the time of this writing it seems quite likely that Haywood will win his other case with Denver as well, which would confirm a basketball player's right to sell his labor to teams in either league.

Not surprisingly, considering the possibility of some real free competition, the two pro basketball leagues are rapidly moving toward a merger that would keep the monopoly intact. The players don't like it one bit. According to Oscar Robertson, the militant black backcourt man who is president of the NBA Players' Association, the players are fully prepared to take whatever legal steps may be necessary to block the merger. A players' strike is also possible. There is also some opposition to the merger in Congress, led by Senator Sam Ervin, the chairman of the Senate Anti-

Trust and Monopoly Subcommittee, and Congressman Emanuel Celler. "With the exception of the United States Government," Ervin told the president of the American Basketball Association, "which can draft people to serve in the services, there is no other business that can draft employees except professional sports. Now a man can get two bids, one from each league [NBA and ABA respectively]. You want him to only be able to get one bid. You say you're doing this for the entertainment of the public. That's exactly what they said in Rome at the Coliseum." (New York *Daily News*, November 16, 1971.)

Another interesting case in which a player faced up to the power of the monopolists and forced them to back down was that of Jim Ninowski, the former Cleveland Browns and Detroit Lions quarterback. In May 1966, when the American and National Football Leagues were supposedly in heated competition for players, Nino was offered about four hundred thousand dollars by the Oakland Raiders to play out his option with the Cleveland Browns and then play three seasons with the Raiders. Why an AFL team felt it had to respect the NFL's option clause is not entirely clear. Ninowski told his NFL owner about the offer, and then after a little time had passed, according to Bernie Parrish (*They Call It a Game*, p. 226 ff.), "He was told that a temporary truce had been arranged between the leagues and that the deal they had agreed on was off." Nino decided to file an anti-trust action against the two leagues. At first he was threatened, but since the NFL was anxious not to have its collusion with the "rival" AFL dragged through the courts and press, he was eventually *paid off in full,* with one hundred thousand dollars a year for four years. After that, Parrish says, Nino was blacklisted by the owners. "Players have been blacklisted for a lot less than taking four hundred thousand dollars out of their tight fists," he adds.

Parrish has offered his own alternative to private monopolistic ownership of teams and players:

> The franchises should be owned by municipal corporations legally tied to the stadium authorities, having public common-stock ownership, with stock being offered to season-ticket holders on the basis of first refusal . . . a formula could be worked out to pay the players a percentage of the total income. Then the profits after expenses could be earmarked for the revitalization of the inner cities—improved wages for police, firemen, teachers, and other civil servants; upgrading of city and county hospitals, and care for the aged; to name a few recipients. (Ibid., p. 290.)

And there would be no "option clause." Under the present system there is not the remotest chance that even this limited plan will be adopted. On the other hand, there is at present no good reason why the players' associations in all of the professional sports could not simply take *control* of their sports—rent stadiums, sell tickets, and divide up the profits among themselves. The present owners perform no worthwhile or necessary function whatever. (And the only injuries they get from the game are the arm strains accumulated raking in the profits.) Instead of the vulture's share of the take, these owners should be paid what they deserve for the amount of work they do—absolutely nothing. If the players' associations in the different sports were able to get together with each other in a professional athletes' union, and then approach other progressive labor unions for support, they would immensely strengthen their ability to win total players' control of sports. Which would, of course, serve as an excellent example for workers' control in industry generally.

Upon the fields of friendly strife
Are sown the seeds
That, upon other fields, on other days,
Will bear the fruits of victory.
General of the Army Douglas MacArthur

5

Molding the Modern Militarist

Lenin pointed out that the monopolistic phase of capitalism is identical with imperialism, since the domestic monopolies require huge quantities of cheap foreign resources, foreign markets, and investment outlets. Monopoly capitalism and imperialism are just the domestic and foreign sides of the same coin. They are linked together by the increasing intervention of the state apparatus both in the domestic monopolies and the foreign markets. Militarism is the heavy-handed tool by which foreign interventions are supported and domestic workers are kept in line. Ideological weapons, such as militarized sports, are also important, and closely linked with nationalism, militarism, and imperialism. The periods of expansion for monopoly capitalism at home are also its periods of imperialist expansion abroad, and it is not difficult to correlate these periods with the rise of the American sports industry.

There have been at least four main periods of business expansion in the past century, both for sports and for the rest of American industry. Each of these followed a major imperialist war. The first boom followed the Civil War, a war in which the markets and raw materials of the South were brought firmly under the imperializing heel of the northern industrial bourgeoisie. The wartime period was marked by a growing appreciation of the importance of physical fitness to developing a winning army. In the years that followed the Napoleonic wars the connection between gymnasium sport and successful warfare was popularized by J. F. Jahn in Germany, and later became an integral part of Prussian militarism, credited by many with toughening the nation for its victory in the Franco-Prussian War of 1871. Following France's defeat, French nationalists, including Baron de Coubertin (later hailed as the founder of the modern Olympic Games) "sought to convince ruling elites that sport for the masses had paramilitary value." (Richard D. Mandell, *The Nazi Olympics*, New York: Macmillan, 1971, p. xii.) The ideas of Jahn, De Coubertin and others gradually gained currency among American educators and army men, and student-organized sports teams in American high schools began to gain increasing favor after the Civil War.

Also immediately following the war in America, reports John Rickards Betts, "the nation felt a new sporting impulse and began to give enthusiastic support to the turf, the diamond, the ring, and other outdoor activities. The game of baseball, spreading from cities to towns and villages, became a national fad, and matches were scheduled with distant communities." (Kenyon and Loy, op. cit., p. 148.) Within five years of the war's end, the first professional baseball league had been formed. Another five years later, in 1876, the National League was founded. The late 1860s and the 1870s also saw the first college football games and the first tennis exhibitions.

This sudden upsurge of sports activity after the war was certainly not just a simple result of the spread of militarist ideology. In part, it was a result of the rapid pace of war-stimulated technology (which led to rapid improvements in railroads, telegraph, underwater cable, cameras, and increasingly rapid mass production— including the beginnings of a mass-production sports industry). Even more important, the post-war prosperity attained by the North led to a tremendous amount of capital investment in rail transport, and it was the existence of these railroads that made intercity games possible. "Baseball clubs made use of the rapidly expanding network of the 1870s," says Betts, "and the organization of the National League in 1876 was only possible with the continued development of the connecting lines." Similarly with horse racing. "The completion of the Pacific Railroad will not be without effect upon the blood stock interests of the great West," declared *Turf, Field and Farm* (New York, I, September 2, p. 69) in 1865. And the following year, the Harlem, Rensselaer, and Saratoga railroad was shipping race horses at cost from New York to Saratoga, which both encouraged the sport and eventually led to increased profits for the line.

The rapid rise of professional boxing following the Civil War was perhaps much more directly due to war-induced fighting temperament. But here, too, despite the illegality of the sport at that time, post-war railroad capital played an important part. Betts notes that when Aaron Jones met Mike McCoole at Busenbark Station, Ohio, in 1867 "tickets were openly sold for excursion trains to the bout." Another big McCoole fight in 1869 induced local railroads to put on all sorts of special trains to bring fans in from Cincinnati and other nearby cities. Similarly, the first college football game between Princeton and Rutgers in 1869 was made possible in part by "the jerky little engine that steamed out of Princeton on the memorable morning of November 6, 1869." (Parke H. Davis, *Football, the American Intercollegiate Game*, New York, 1911, p. 45.)

War-speeded technology also led to the successful laying of the Atlantic cable by Cyrus Field in 1866. This, in turn, led to a tremendous expansion in reporting of English sporting events on this side of the Atlantic—particularly of horse-racing results, which formerly took up to three weeks to get here—which, in turn, encouraged similar sport exhibitions over here. By the end of 1866 James Gordon Bennett's New York *Herald* was featuring cabled dispatches of the great ocean race. And by 1869 the crew race between Harvard and Oxford was being transmitted across the Atlantic cable to provide news for countless American papers. Also, cheap production methods that came in following the war led to a tremendous expansion in dime sports novels and athletic almanacs. The largest producer of these was the New York firm of Beadle & Adams. One of the standard ploys in these novels— whether they discussed the war, the Wild West, or the emerging world of sports—was the creation of a supervirile hero figure whose exploits would then be eagerly followed by his fans. War heroes merged into sports heroes. And the conception of the hero figure in American life gradually assumed increasing importance. It served as a prop for "survival of the fittest" notions of social Darwinism that became current in succeeding decades, and also for more general notions of class and racial elitism that were prevalent at the time. Just as the All-American sports hero was destined to clobber the opposition, so the military hero of the General Custer variety was justified in clobbering the Indians. The hero deserved to win. God was on his side.

During the years of the "new" British and French

imperialist penetration into Africa and the Far East
in the 1880s and early 1890s, American investments
abroad had risen substantially and had effected a steady
flow of foreign dividends into this country. The 1880s
brought the tremendous boom in popularity of professional boxing in the John L. Sullivan era, and closed
with the first golf matches. The 1890s featured the invention of basketball in 1891, and the first modern
Olympic Games in 1896 (the latter being Baron de
Coubertin's method of toughening up French youth for
another possible war with Germany and, hence, was
another fallout from the Franco-German war of 1871).
But in America, too, sports was marching in lock step
with militarism. The year 1893 witnessed the first great
wave of agitation to annex Hawaii. The Spanish-
American War of 1898 marked the open development
of American monopoly capitalism into global imperialism. It ended with the U. S. in political control
of Puerto Rico and the Philippines, and economic control of Cuba. In the post-war boom that followed, the
American League was formed. By 1901 Congress had
passed the Platt Amendment, establishing an economic
protectorate over Cuba, and the U. S. was also pushing
the "open door" policy to get a foothold for our trade
in China. (This was the year the American League
opened for business.)

Just as the prosperity of the post-Civil War era had
produced a capital investment boom in railroads, so the
post-Spanish-American War era produced a burgeoning
auto industry. The advertising approach of the new
industry turned out to be the new "sport" of auto racing, created by the manufacturers themselves to hawk
their product in the late 1890s. After Henry Ford
managed to win a big race against Alexander Winton
in Detroit in 1902, "Ford's prowess as a 'speed demon'
began to appear in the columns of the widely circulated trade journal *Horseless Age*." (Keith Sward, *The
Legend of Henry Ford*, New York, Rinehart, 1948, p.

14.) Ford later claimed in his autobiography that auto racing "brought advertising of the only kind that people cared to read." (Henry Ford and Samuel Crowther, *My Life and Work,* Garden City, 1927, p. 37.) He added, "A week after the [Winton] race I formed the Ford Motor Company."

Big American manufacturing industries such as autos required foreign raw materials, markets, and investment outlets. The year 1903 saw the Hay-Vorilla treaty finalizing our plunder of Columbia, and giving American capital a perpetual lease on the Panama Canal. The Canal was actually completed in 1914 (the year the abortive Federal baseball League was founded). At about the same time, the United States invaded Haiti and Mexico and launched the first of several invasions of Nicaragua. (Four years earlier we had clamped down on the economies of Costa Rica and Honduras.) In 1916 the marines invaded the Dominican Republic, and the next year the army penetrated Mexico again. This pattern of outright invasions and economic blockades symbolized the growing importance of foreign investments and dividends to the developing monopoly capitalist economy. By 1914 U. S. investment abroad had reached $3.5 billion, as compared to $500 million in 1900, and by 1930 it was $17 billion. In the post-World War I boom, the flow of foreign earnings back into the U. S. and the new investment opportunities abroad provided one of the material bases for a tremendous expanison of American business, including the developing sports business.

The founding of the National Hockey League in Canada took place in 1917, and in 1926 it expanded to include some of the major American cities. In 1920 the National Football League was founded. The early 1920s also saw the mass construction of stadiums and boxing arenas. And by the second half of the decade the "golden era" of American sports was under way. This third big expansion in sports was tremendously aided by the development of the new mass media of radio in the '20s. And once again the groundwork for the expansion was helped along by increasing population (from 76 million in 1900 to 105.7 million in 1920), increasing urbanization (from 39.7 per cent to 51.3 per cent), increased rail transport (from 193,000 miles of track to 260,000), and the huge increase in economic surplus generally, due in part to imperialist investments abroad. It is also worth noting that during the period from 1860 to 1920, the work week dropped from sixty-six hours per week to about fifty, and real wages nevertheless jumped by about 75 per cent, thus providing both the increased leisure and increased spending money necessary to create the booming sports attendances of the late '20s.

The next big bonus for the sports world was to be World War II. As the war drew closer in Europe, the Conservatives in England introduced what was to be the Physical Training and Recreation Bill of 1937, providing calisthenics for all school children in order to get the nation in shape for future conflict. (Similarly in Canada, the onset of war led to the passage of the 1943 Physical Fitness Act.) At the time many unfavorably compared this dreary regimen of physical exercises to be imposed on working-class kids with the team sports being played in the elite English public schools. "This idea that you must get all the boys and girls in rows, like chocolate soldiers," commented Labor MP Aneurin Bevan in the House of Commons, "and make them go through evolutions, is a miserable substitute for giving them sufficient playgrounds in which they can play their own games in their own ways." Still military preparedness was eventually served, and physical education became big business in England.

In America, too, the war era brought a new boom in sports. For example, in his pamphlet entitled "The Sporting Goods Market Outlook . . . is GREAT!," R. E. Snyder of the National Sporting Goods Association traces the rise of the sporting goods industry from its "relative obscurity" before World War II to its expansion by almost 70 per cent the year World War II ended: "The subsequent release from duty of many thousands of servicemen whose training had included volleyball, soccer, and sundry other 'phsycial development' sports activities, provided the spark for enlivenment of the then sluggish sporting goods business." (Similarly, the post-World War I sporting boom had been due in large measure to the development of the first sports programs in the military during that war.) Once again the sports expansion of the late '40s and '50s, was helped along by a tremendous expansion of transportation facilities. Not only were there enough cars to get almost anyone out to the stadium, but there were enough air-line routes—they jumped from 43,000 miles in 1940 to 79,000 by 1955—to get teams around the country and lay the basis for coast-to-coast leagues. (The airplane, of course, had been perfected in both world wars, primarily for bombing purposes.) By the '60s the booming population out on the West Coast provided the market lure for a host of major league teams. And once again, the sports expansion and the general industrial expansion, with which it went hand in hand, were spurred along by the tremendous postwar growth of American imperialist investment abroad, and particularly by the huge expansion of markets, raw materials, and foreign dividends that this produced.[1]

[1] Nkrumah notes that between 1938 and 1948, American exports into the European and Japanese colonial areas jumped from 11 per cent of their net imports to 25 per cent, and America's African trade alone grew from just $150 million to $12,000 million in that period. "Between 1950 and 1959 private American firms invested $4,500 million in the developing countries and made three times as much. Net profits came to $8,300 million to which can be added millions of dollars in trading profits, interests on loans, freight charges, and other ancillary operations." (*Neo-Colonialism*, London: Heinemann, 1965, p. 58.)

At the height of the Cold War, and especially following Russia's launching of the first Sputnik, there
were once again clarion calls that the nation had better get in shape for possible war. John Kennedy made
this his main campaign pitch in the 1960 election,
deftly combining a call for greater physical fitness and
preparedness with calls for better military preparedness
and missiles. Kennedy's election resulted in a big boost
for the long hike, the touch football game, and more
physical training programs in the schools. Similarly in
England, the Wolfenden Commission came up with
proposals (quickly adopted in Parliament) for a Ministry of Sports with a multimillion-dollar budget to
help get that nation in shape for the post-Sputnik demands of the Cold War. As the Vietnam war gathered
momentum, President Johnson, his Secretary of Defense
and various of the Joint Chiefs of Staff started putting
in appearances at major sports events, particularly football bowl games. And then President Nixon developed
the technique of suggesting special football plays before big games and phoning in congratulations to
coaches afterwards. Even more important, as we've
said, the militarization of American society accompanying the Vietnam war led to the replacement of baseball
by the more militarized game of pro football as the
nation's most popular sport.

"God, Country, School and Team" read a placard
put up in the locker room by a leading college football
coach. "Olympic athletes," writes Alex Natan in his
Sport and Society (also reprinted in Kenyon and Loy,
op. cit., p. 203), "have become soldiers of sport who
are indoctrinated with grotesque conceptions of national prestige. . . . Today international competitive
sport has become everywhere—whether openly or
secretly—a propaganda weapon in world affairs which
through the incitement of inherent [?] nationalist in-

stincts points ways and means to new methods of psychological warfare . . ."

As an example of the connection between the imperialist, nationalist, and sporting mentalities, we might consider the February 7, 1965 memo from National Security adviser McGeorge Bundy to then President Lyndon Johnson, calling for an escalation to the war in Vietnam. The memo was revealed and paraphrased by Ralph Stavins, a resident fellow of the Institute of Policy Studies. According to Stavins the memo sized up the U. S. position on the eve of escalation in roughly these terms: "The No. 1 nation, having sent its first team abroad to defend its No. 1 position, was unequivocally obligated to support that team in the face of any threat to it."

Similarly, at a Saigon press conference, Admiral Harry D. Felt was asked a particularly embarrassing question about why his fighting men were losing the war. He turned on his interrogator, and demanded, "Why don't you get on the team!" The reporter, Malcolm Browne of the Associated Press tried hard to get the message. In 1968 he wrote an article noting "[President] Johnson is still at bat, but we're in the ninth inning now, and the home team is still badly behind." Sports fans across America are apparently obligated to support the military "team" with their sons' lives.

In August 1970 in England, the *Financial Times* implied that British Leyland workers have an obligation to support their company "team." The paper quotes the managing director of the firm's Austin Morris division as appealing to returning strikers: "We must *all* buckle down to the job in hand of getting more production out of our factories and producing more efficiently to keep ourselves in competition." (August 3, 1970.)

These examples illustrate the essence of the nationalistic way of thinking: Individuals—or individual classes

—are supposedly obligated to subordinate their particular individual or class interests to the discipline of "their" team. The "team" might be their school, company, city, state, church, race, sex, nation, etc. Our list of possible "teams" is by no means exhaustive, but we can already see that individuals are members of many possible teams. What the nationalist ideologist tries to do is claim that the team he is making a pitch for is so important that "obligations" to it must overshadow other possible identifications and loyalties. Let us see how this works in particular sports-related cases.

A columnist for the Toronto *Telegram* (November 12, 1970) said the following in describing a high school football team: "What impressed me the most was the total dedication of the players to the cause of the school. Without hope of financial reward or making football their career. Some defied injuries to play. Others played on, barely able to crawl." He adds that sex seemed as remote as the *"après ski"* life style of the Alps (in which sex is used as a vehicle for selling skiing and Alpine ski resorts). The columnist seems to feel that it is, beyond any shadow of doubt, a great thing that kids should be taught to sacrifice personal well-being, health, sex, and money for the good of "their" school. But how much is it "their" school when decisions are being made as to what teachers to hire, what courses to give, whether to give grades, what grades and so on?

Similarly, American Presidents used to demand a bipartisan foreign policy on the ground that everyone must stick with the team through thick and thin. And the quarterback calls the signals for the team, right? So when people first started criticizing America's invasion of Vietnam, presidential spokesmen damned them as "Monday morning quarterbacks."

A Toronto *Globe and Mail* columnist (October 1, 1970) quotes one of the players of the local Canadian Football League team: "We sense that some of the fans are letting us down. Yet the fans are part of this team, too. We all must pull together, all of us, 100 per cent, the newspapers and everybody." The columnist himself did not quite buy this argument. He pointed out that, though the local pro football team might provide the fan with entertainment, "it puts no money in his pocket." Indeed, the fans were financially supporting the team owners and stockholders, and the team was not only big business, but "monopolistic big business." The point is that, since the fan does not get an equal stake in choosing "his" team's management or raking in the profits, why should he have to refrain from criticizing, through thick and thin, the results of the management's decisions. In what sense, then, was it "his" team?

Writing in Natan's book, *Sport and Society*, Renee Haynes has noted that, "It is chiefly through sport (at any rate in peace time) that male industrial workers can submerge themselves, if only as roaring spectators, in the communal will that 'their' team, the group with which they are identified, should win." The real question, of course, is whether workers should submerge their class identity in "their" team—be it a sports team, a corporation, or a nation—especially as they have no really effective control over its policies or profits.

What about the argument that class identity or loyalty is just another kind of "team spirit"? In a sense, this is perfectly true. And there is certainly nothing wrong with team spirit and co-operation among people. In fact, it is essential to building any kind of democratic society. However, in a society where a small percentage of the population owns essentially all of the wealth and does almost none of the work, it is a bit misleading to claim that we're all on the same "team." We certainly don't all have an equal stake in "our team." Nor an equal voice in deciding its policies. And so, too, with the company team, the military team, the school team, the university community, ad infinitum. The call for these misplaced varieties of team spirit amounts to an

ideological attack on the group self-interest of the least
wealthy and powerful groups in our society. It calls on
them to accept their inferior position "for the sake of
the team." Every day workers are enjoined and encouraged by the mass media to think of themselves as
"fans" of a particular team, or as "Americans," or as
"consumers," or as "tax payers," or as everything and
anything but workers who spend 100 per cent of their
working lives taking orders from bosses. In other words,
they are being asked to identify with every team but
the real team, the only team in the only contest that
can really make a difference—workers versus capitalists.
By this standard, class loyalty is a very different sort of
team spirit in that it is actually based on the real objective self-interest of each working person for an equal
stake in the nation, city, company, or whatever. By
comparison, identification with sports teams is at best
escapist, and for a worker to identify with his "company team" or "the nation's military team" might well
run *against* his true interests. It goes without saying that
a worker who is so busy rooting for the Yankees that
he forgets that his real wages are declining is a good
bet to be so busy rooting for the Yanks in Vietnam that
he forgets that his son might get killed there. And it is
only when workers get so enamored of their "national
team" that they can be induced to kill workers of other
countries so that their bosses can continue to make
profits.

It seems, unfortunately, to be true that many workers *can* be duped into worrying about "their" team,
even as their houses rot or their kids begin to get
hungry. In 1969, when the Mets won the World Series,
New York went wild, and Mayor Lindsay was able to
use this tremendous "success" in his re-election campaign. Living conditions continued to get worse, but
the people had their opium.

We had the same thing with the Dodgers and the
Giants in the '50s. As the city continued to fall apart,

the fans simply closed their eyes and concentrated instead on the pennants "their" teams were giving them. Then the bosses decided they could make bigger profits in California. Some fans never did figure out what happened to "their" teams.

Herbert Marcuse has recently pointed out (Toronto *Star*, May 30, 1972) that a necessary condition for the development of nationalism is the belief in an external enemy. This is clearly as true for high school nationalism as it is for the patriotism of nation states. And learning to root for the home team, and boo the "enemy" team, is an important socialization device by which this nationalistic mentality is developed. There is nothing accidental about this. For the past half century American high school principals have justified inflated athletic budgets with avowals that the "school spirit" learned by rooting for the school team is a valuable building block for the "national spirit" necessary to weld together what is usually called a great nation.

Of course, in the troubled racial climate of recent years the scholarly appeals for "school spirit" from the principals have turned increasingly sour. In former decades high school nationalisms and rivalries with the "enemy" school had only evolved to the point where fights between the two groups of spectators could more or less be avoided by seating each school's boosters on opposite sides of the field or court on which the game was being played. True, one school's fans might make an occasional foray into the "enemy" school's fan section, and an occasional fight might break out. But it was usually not too serious, and most often could be dismissed as a kind of athletic panty raid. In the racial turbulence of the late '60s, however, at a time when *de facto* segregation of city schools was still the rule rather than the exception, spectator rivalries at athletic contests between predominantly black and predominantly white high schools assumed an increasingly ugly and racist character. What had previously been

laughed off as "school spirit," openly assumed the guise
and bitterness of race nationalism. In New York City,
for example, it was often insufficient merely to separate
the two groups of boosters (even with armed security
patrols in between). Many high school basketball
games had, literally, to be played *in secret*, with no
spectators allowed in at all, lest "school spirit" ignite
with racism to lead to interscholastic warfare.

Few people realize just how much this sort of "Our
Team versus The Opponents" thinking has penetrated
into all aspects of our conception of the world. Take
the news that gets printed in our newspapers, or indeed
the very concept of news. There's an old saying among
reporters about which happenings deserve to be
called "news": It goes, "conflict is news." If there isn't
as much overt conflict in a report of a student strike or
a parade as there would be in, say, a football game, the
news is often rewritten to get more in. The stereotyped
clashes of Good versus Evil are familiar enough. The
Free World versus Communist Aggression. Cautious
Executives versus Irresponsible Strikers. Dignified Professors versus Excitable Students. In short, Our Team
versus The Enemy. (And, if you look closely, you will
find that every news story of this kind carries a neat
little string of adjectives like moderate and militant,
mainstream and extremist, straight and left wing, and
so on, just to tell you which is Our Team and which
The Enemy.) Sometimes it looks as if the values and
stereotypes of the sports page have come to dominate
the whole paper. But this is only superficially true, for
the question arises: Where do the values of the sports
page originate? As we've seen, monopoly capital, by
reserving the lion's share of the wealth for those at the
top, encourages the fiercest "survival of the fittest" type
competition of those at the bottom. And it makes use of
a distorted hypercompetitive sports ideology to facilitate this hypercompetition. Moreover, it finds it necessary to mobilize everyone against the External Enemy

of the day (both to knit together a monopoly-dominated nation at home and justify the plunder of neo-colonial countries abroad). This is the real reason why *both* the sports and the rest of the news have to be militarized and presented as competitions between totally opposed moral stereotypes. With God on "our side."

Many people who would, perhaps, concede that identification with sports teams is a socializer for the sort of false consciousness that leads workers to submerge their class interest in a mythical "national interest" (even if it means dying for their bosses). But few people realize that this connection between sports nationalism and national chauvinism is much more than an accident. It is a connection of which our rulers have always been aware, and which they have never ceased to push. It is, in fact, one of the central reasons for the Establishment's support of sports, without which the place of organized athletics might be much less than it is.

In England the connection between team sports and building a national consciousness was popularized in the novels of Thomas Hughes, especially in his *Tom Brown's School Days*. Hughes pushed the view that cricket was more or less the birthright of all right-thinking, bourgeois Englishmen, young or old, and the thing that distinguished the British from other peoples. "Give me a boy who is a cricketer," declared the Headmaster of Winchester in 1860. "I can make something of him." (P. C. McIntosh, *Sport in Society*, London: Alden and Mowbray, 1963.) Namely, a right-thinking English gentleman.

Baron Pierre de Coubertin, the founder of the modern Olympics, who is usually depicted by sports historians as some sort of saint concerned with the welfare of mankind, was, as we've said, a French jingoist, nursing a grudge against Germany for defeating France in 1871, and seeing his international meets as a way of toughening up French youth for future military engagements. Richard D. Mandell (op. cit.) points out that De Coubertin saw international competition as a good way of "reinvigorating" the French nation.

In *Sport in Society*, McIntosh notes that the team games of the nineteenth century "encouraged just those qualities of co-operation and conformity to the needs of the herd which were so much prized by a middle class which was establishing its power and influence throughout the world." (Here, "middle class" signifies the industrial bourgeoisie, as contrasted with the landed aristocracy.) Deputy Editor Peregrine Worsthorne, writing in the London *Sunday Telegraph*, recently wrote about how the race of imperialists who built the British Empire was formed on the playing fields of Harrow and Eton. There has never been any great secret about this. Capitalists, clerics, and military men of all stripes have long spoken openly about the usefulness of British sports to building British character, British sentiment, and British imperialism. So had it been with Jahn, the father of Prussian militarism in Germany. So it was with De Coubertin. So it was with Hitler.

So it is today. Only a few years ago a government Task Force on Sports for Canadians, consisting of former Great Canadian Oil Sands, Ltd., chairman Harold Rea and Olympic ski champ Nancy Greene (a perfect marriage of the worlds of sports and big business), noted that though they could not weigh precisely the contribution of sports in knitting together the Canadian nation, "it must have been considerable," and has "continuing significance" in keeping "an intrinsically Canadian sense of community" in the face of American nationalism. "Sport is one of the few dimensions of Canadian life," they say, "in which truly national folk heroes have been created, and are constantly being created." Sport has been "a psychological nation builder." So, like the Wolfenden Commission in

England, they recommended that there be a government agency of sport with millions of dollars at its disposal to push this builder of national consciousness: "Our point is that we must *create* the aspiration in millions of young Canadians in the years ahead that the objective of their sporting ambition is to play on a *national* team [my italics]." (Report of the Task Force on Sports for Canadians, Ottawa, 1969.)

From the 1880s through the first half of this century the thing that melted all the immigrants into one stadium and gave every boy a chance to become—if not President—well, at least another Jackie Robinson, was baseball. This was the *National* Pastime. Every game started with our National Anthem. And even the leagues were the *National* League and the *American* League. This was obviously Americanism in action. It was "un-American" to criticize it. In the more militarized seventies, football has become the National Shrine. Fittingly, Utah State football coach Chuck Mills designed a red, white, and blue flag decal for his team's helmets, and then told his "troops": "This decal means football is the great American game. It is a game where you sacrifice, respect each other and yourself, work together regardless of backgrounds and political, social or religious beliefs for a common goal . . . Football is a micro-form of the American Adventure."

In Canada the big nation builder has been ice hockey. "It ties together all generations and all classes in a common interest," says Canadian Broadcasting Corporation script writer Jack Hutchinson. "Hockey is not only Canada's national sport," says the patriotic and unbiased G. E. Mara (who was president of the Toronto Maple Leafs), "it is a way of life of countless citizens [?], young and old, and beyond doubt, contributes in a multitude of ways to the building of young men, to the social structure and to the basic fiber of our people." Notice the names of the three Canadian teams in the National Hockey League—the Maple Leafs (Canada's national symbol and the emblem on its Flag), the Canadiens, and the Canucks. All three names have been deliberately chosen to appeal to a capital-N Nationalist consciousness. The name "Montreal Canadiens" is particularly offensive to many in Montreal, which is smack in the middle of French-speaking Quebec. "This is just one more symbol of Quebec's subjection to English Canada," said one Montrealer. "The team should have been called the 'Quebecois.'" So hockey has become kind of a rallying point for French nationalist consciousness and against what is perceived as English Canadian imperialism.

This is not the first time a neo-colony has used sports in this way. Sukarno built his Stadium of the Emerging Peoples in Indonesia. And Nkrumah was at work on a similar project in Ghana. In a host of the Balkanized countries of Latin America, international soccer rivalries between the different states (especially in the World Cup) provide almost the only rallying point for the perpetuation of the various nationalisms. Here, of course, we see how absurd nationalism can be, because it keeps these Latin states divided and weak and, hence, easy prey to U. S. economic imperialism.

Sports have also been used to cement empires together. The Romans popularized chariot races and gladiatorial combat in all parts of their empire. And the British encouraged cricket and rugby throughout theirs. One can still have the depressing experience of visiting some black African or West Indian state and watching the locals play cricket. And even today the old Tory imperialists in Britain are fighting hard to maintain their country's cricket and rugby ties with South Africa. Of course, no sooner did the American Army occupy Japan after World War II, than they started pushing baseball. Our rulers sell their nationalist ideology with their sports both at home and abroad.

The era of imperialism obviously requires, first and foremost, a strong military apparatus. Sports fields have been traditional nurturing grounds for building the kind of men needed to police an empire. This, in turn, requires citizen soldiers who have been well-socialized into conforming to a militarized view of reality. One of the simplest ways by which the military world view is smuggled into sports is through the very words used to describe the contest. Today, if you tune in to the football game you might hear such things as "the *offensive* (or *attacking*) *formation* . . . the *guards* protecting the *field general* . . . who unleashes *the bomb* . . . sends a man on a *dive* (*smashing, driving, slicing*) through the *enemy line* . . . and the *defense* is *blasting* in with a *blitz* . . . there's an *interception* . . ." In fact, what used to be called the "single wing" formation emerged in the Vietnam war years as the "shot gun offense." The heroes commonly have names like "Pistol Pete," "Bullet Bob," "Boomer," or "Cannonball." Or if you switch over to baseball, you might hear: "On the mound a *flame-throwing* right-hander . . . *fires* it in . . . and he *blasts* it out of the park . . . a tremendous *smash* . . ." Moreover in these militarized times nobody simply "wins." One side always kills, clobbers, smashes, smothers, beats, belts, blasts, or what have you, the other. In fact, the very words used to make sports headlines serve equally well to describe warfare: "Yanks Crush Tribe," "West Stomps East," "Army Rolls Over Navy," etc. Long-time NHL coach "Punch" Imlach even wrote a book entitled *Hockey Is a Battle*.

Throughout recorded history, sports and warfare have been to varying degrees inseparable. War has been regarded as a sport—the "Sport of Kings" according to Huizinga. And sports have been seen as a kind of mock war. Max Rafferty, former State Superintendent of Public Instruction in California and a former high school football coach, told a Rotary Club gathering that football is "war—without killing." And, similarly,

Nazi General von Reichenau described it as "war with friendly arms." For hundreds of years sports were regarded as a prelude to, or preparation for, actual war. The first sports, now called "blood sports," were merely a mirror image of the sort of encounters that took place on the battle field, and the Ancient Greek word *agon*—meaning a test of valor, match, or contest—has survived in English in the form of "agonistic"—i.e., contending—or, perhaps more pointedly, as "agony." Even when things had evolved to the stage of the Greek Olympiads, the sorts of competition emphasized were still skills like speed or javelin throwing, which would be useful in battle. Similarly, the jousting tournaments of medieval knights were a kind of mock warfare, and the training that preceded them was regarded, more or less explicitly, as training for battle. And we have the Duke of Wellington's testimony that "Waterloo was won on the playing fields of Eton."

From an economic standpoint, the maintenance of a huge army or a huge sports industry are similar in that both manage to waste a vast amount of what might otherwise be productive labor. Veblen, in his book *Imperial Germany and the Industrial Revolution* (Ann Arbor: University of Michigan Press, 1968), apparently never conceived that the economic surplus would be large enough, or the need to militarize society great enough, to have both industries booming concurrently. So he concentrated on distinguishing between the militarism of Imperial Prussia and the pseudo militarism of English sports, and presented these as *alternative* ways of moronizing the working class and inculcating them with the habits of subordination. Today we know better. With a larger economic surplus available for unproductive—and destructive—activities, both kinds of brainwashing can go on at once and reinforce one another.

Army's 1961 quarterback, Dick Eckert, when interviewed by the Associated Press in Vietnam where he was a first lieutenant, remarked that there is a lot in common in playing sports and being in battle. "There's the same tension," he insisted, "the same feeling. All the training is like practicing in sports. You've got to train. You develop the same type of team work that you do in battle. When the going gets tough, the tough get going [the old Army football battle cry]."

Gene Ward, the well-known flag-waving sports columnist for the New York *Daily News* once pointed out in an article headed "Football Pays High Dividends in Battle" that, when you dug into the records, you found that a startling number of America's leading generals and admirals "first learned to defend their land on a tiny patch of gridiron turf." And that later when they had to defend their country in World War II and the Cold War, "this defense of America which they chose was strictly according to the best American tradition that a good offense is the best defense, no where more aptly exhibited than in the game of football." And, predictably, his main example of this is, "The most offensive-minded general of them all— George Smith Patton, the two-gun, two-fisted fighter who mounted the armored assaults which outblitzed Hitler's blitz boys." He quotes Col. Meade Wildrick, a classmate of "Old Blood and Guts" at West Point, that the great general "used to play football like he did everything else—with rambunctious aggressiveness."

Ward notes that General Eisenhower also played football at West Point in 1913, served as coach of the freshman team in 1914, and that his special talents were speed and ability to diagnose plays, "the same speed of judgment and ability to call plays which took us [sic] into Berlin [forgetting that it was the Russian Army that captured Berlin]."

In his later years, General Eisenhower was quoted by Soviet writer A. Kuleshov as having admitted that, "the true mission of American sports is to prepare young people for war." (Morton, op. cit., p. 109.)

Seated with Ike in a 1915 photo of graduating West
Point football lettermen were generals-to-be Vernon
Prichard (later an armor division commander in Italy),
Millard Harmon (later to command the 6th and 13th
Air Forces), commander-to-be of the 84th Infantry
Roscoe Woodruff, James Van Fleet (one of the leaders
of Ike's Normandy invasion team), Leland Hobbs
(commander of the 30th Infantry), Thomas Larkin
(later commanding general of services and supply for
the   Mediterranean),   and   Brigadier-General-to-be
Walter Hess. And, such World War II admirals as
"Bull" Halsey, Ingram, King, Land, and "Bullet Bob"
Ghormley won their football laurels at Navy. Army
Chief of Staff, and later Secretary of State, George C.
Marshall, once compared the planning of war to quar-
terbacking a football team. (He got his warm-up for
the big team at Virginia Military College, where he
made the All-Southern Conference as a tackle.)
Official West Point figures released in 1945 showed
that between 1890 and 1945, of the 513 cadets who
had won varsity football letters, no less than 89 had
(by that date) already achieved the rank of brigadier
general or higher!

Before the 1966 Army-Navy game, Townsend
Clarke, the Army captain, received the following
telegram:

THE BYWORD OF ALL WEST POINTERS IN VIETNAM IS
QUOTE BEAT NAVY, UNQUOTE BEST OF LUCK. [SIGNED]
GENERAL W. C. WESTMORELAND AND THE LONG GRAY
LINE IN VIETNAM

Discussing the telegram with the Philadelphia *In-
quirer*, Clarke noted quietly, "Everybody's going to the
Far East, sir, in time. I'm partial to the infantry. I like
rugged-type leadership." He had obviously learned his
lessons well, and General Westmoreland himself
would certainly have understood. Major General Norman Edwards, who played for Army in the '30s, re-

cently recalled that among the football "scrubs" of his day were Westmoreland, Abrams (Westmoreland's successor as commander in Vietnam) Throckmorton (formerly deputy commander in Vietnam), and "others who have gone on to great heights."

Whatever one thinks of these great heights, there is no doubt that the Vietnam war has gone hand in hand with a tremendous increase in the popularity of football, a game which the late Vinnie Lombardi, when he was coaching the militarized mastodons of the Green Bay Packers, described as nothing but discipline. Lombardi himself, both as a slave-driving coach and as a leading exponent of the application of military methods to civilian life generally, summed up in his own personality and views the rabid authoritarianism so characteristic of today's big-time sports. "The individual," he once said, "has to have respect for authority regardless of what that authority is. I think the individual has gone too far. I think ninety-five per cent of the people, as much as they shout, would rather be led than lead." And in the next breath he added, "Everywhere you look, there is a call for freedom, independence or whatever you wish to call it. But as much as these people want to be independent, they still want to be told what to do . . ." So we all need our football coaches, managers, drill sergeants, and occasionally a good war, just to toughen us up. Lombardi, fittingly, got his college coaching start as a backfield coach for Army in the late '40s and later moved up to direct the hard-hitting offense of the New York Giants before moving on to command the Packers. He whipped his players along with tongue-lashing personal abuse, brutal training sessions, callousness, and absolute discipline. He was a bitter opponent of the efforts of National Football League players to form a union, and on the subject of collective bargaining he once declared, "If they come here as a group, they will go right out as a group." Nor was he loathe to put this into practice. When the players staged a boycott of training in 1968 to win a better pension scheme, Lombardi and other football execs answered it with a lockout.

A few months before he died in 1970, he served as vice-chairman of the July Fourth Honor America Day, a thinly disguised pro-war rally concocted by such people as Bob Hope and Billy Graham to "support our boys in Vietnam." Green Bay's All-Pro center, Jim Ringo, used to say that when the team lined up, as far as he was concerned, it was the Free World on their side of the ball, and the Communists on the other. And even as the great coach lay on his deathbed, he still managed to scramble up for a meeting of club owners to tell the brass not to give in to any further demands of the players' association. Mike Jay of the *Daily World* remarked, "There wasn't a dry millionaire's eye in the place when the great Lombardi told them not to be pushed around by a bunch of kids." Predictably, when this great military figure died, he got reams of front-page coverage, TV specials, and a flag-waving funeral, complete with Cardinal Cooke and a eulogy from the President of the United States.

Lombardi's players often compared his methods to those of General Patton. And even college coaches copied them. And when you're in a war with a General Patton for your commander, injuries mean nothing. ("Nobody is hurt," Lombardi used to say. "Hurt is in your mind. If you can walk you can run.") In his book *Out of Their League* Dave Meggyesy points out that few college football players escape without some form of permanent disability. "During my four years," he noted, "I accumulated a broken wrist, separations of both shoulders, an ankle that was torn up so badly it broke the arch of my foot, three major brain concussions, and an arm that almost had to be amputated because of improper treatment, and I was one of the lucky ones." In his *Farewell to Football*, Jerry Kramer

tells how he learned he had a detached retina in his
eye just before the championship game of the 1960
season. He'd been playing with this injury for three
quarters of the season. The doctor advised against playing in the strongest possible terms. "Jerry, this can make
you blind," he said. "It's very serious." Kramer replied,
"So's the game." He was allowed to play. He did. Then
he had his operation, was bandaged and blindfolded
for days, while his sight hung in the balance. "The experience should have scared me out of football," he
admits. The doctor strongly advised against playing any
more. "I'm going to play," he insisted. "I've got to play."
He was lucky. At the back of his book, the publishers
give a list of Kramer's serious football injuries. It goes
on for almost two pages. "He's spent more time taped
up, hospitalized, or coaxing wounds to heal than he
has playing football." No doubt all this can be pointed
to as an outstanding example of the "courage" of a
gridiron gladiator. An example of "heart." I call it
socialization in militarized madness.

A great deal has been written by such ideologues
as David Reisman, William Whyte, and Vance
Packard about the transformation of our generals and
industrial managers from an individualistic, inner-
directed, hard-driving, competitive Protestant work
ethic to an other-directed, non-competitive, organization man, social ethic of co-operation and harmony.
(The ideologies of the industrial bourgeoisie in their
competitive and monopolistic phases.) And at first sight
it might seem surprising that team sports were able to
cope with these changing socialization requirements.
How does one produce both co-operative capitalists
(oligopolists) and hypercompetitive workers on the
same sports fields? And how can one use sports to produce industrial managers and military officers who are
both competitive and co-operative, both personally acquisitive and team-oriented?

It helps to look at the problem in its class framework. At one end of the spectrum we have the sort of comparatively relaxed sports played by ruling-class sons in Ivy League colleges. The players have been recruited, for the most part, from the elite Eastern prep schools. And since there is no plethora of candidates for the team, they have comparatively little competition for starting positions. Therefore, while winning is pleasant, it is not made hyperimportant. Gentlemanliness holds sway over aggressiveness. And team play is distinctly more important than personal competitiveness. This corresponds to the situation for ruling-class sons. They have it made—and don't have to compete too hard.

At the other end of the class spectrum we have, say, the black scholarship athlete at a Big Ten or West Coast state university, or the rookie in a professional team's training camp. Here potential players for every position are a dime a dozen. So competition for jobs is incredibly fierce. (Particularly for those black athletes who find themselves "stacked" at certain positions like running backs, defensive backs, and tackles in football—where they have to compete against other blacks under what is a de facto quota system for starting jobs.) Here gentlemanliness and co-operation between job rivals is entirely a myth. Aggressiveness is everything. And though mock obeisance is made to teamwork, the scarcity of jobs ensures that almost everyone is going on the old ethic of "what's in it for me?" This corresponds to the situation of industrial workers in a society in which one fifth of the population controls four fifths of the wealth, and the remaining four fifths of the people are forced to compete fiercely for only one fifth of the wealth they produce.

In between the capitalists at the top and the workers at the bottom we have the industrial managers. Or in the state apparatus, in between the ruling-class politicians and the lower grades of the army and the civil service, we get the professional army men and civil servants. (In England, they'd be likely to get their college degrees at London University rather than Oxford.) This is the strata of the ruling class at which the opposing pressures toward co-operativeness and competitiveness (Reisman calls it "antagonistic co-operation"), team play and personal acquisitiveness, clash most forcefully. Football, more than any other sport, forces the same sort of contradictory socialization pressures on the player. Interestingly, a recent *Fortune* magazine survey showed that 78.9 per cent of young managers watch football on television. According to Michael Maccoby of the Institute for Policy Studies in Washington:

> First, the player must be co-operative with his teammates. But he must also be out to win, i.e., to beat out others for his job on the team as well as to crush the opposition. His aggressiveness and competitiveness, thus, must be controlled. In the corporation, this control is in part achieved by setting limited goals, to be met within a particular time period. The player must also be able to turn himself on and off, so to speak . . . Nor should he put personal concerns ahead of the organizational goal, the advancement of the team . . . This syndrome of traits— which can be called the game character—is of inestimable value for building both winning teams and organizations . . . ("Some Hypotheses on Technology and Character in the Modern Industrial Organization," Chicago: American Association for the Advancement of Science, 1970.)

Thus our middle-range managers acquire the schizoid "game characters" that enable them to do their jobs.

It is, of course, true that when the working class was finally allotted the time and extra wages necessary to engage in sports, they took out of this the discipline and narcotized habits of minds that enabled them to

function in the lower levels of the army or on the assembly lines. But the workers never attended such pe-
culiarly *all-male* institutions as prep schools or military
academies, with all the overtones of repressed homo-
sexuality, with the absolute heterosexual repression
characteristic of a prison or a convent, and predictably
producing in abundance the same fever pitch of sado-
masochism necessary to work up to an industrial or military command role. Anyone who reads Vance Packard's
book *The Pyramid Climbers* or William Whyte's por-
trait of *The Organization Man* cannot doubt that there
is something incredibly masochistic about all the pun-
ishment our industrial and military leaders are willing
to take to come up through the ranks to top levels of
the managerial ladder. No one need be surprised that
such people become slave-driving sadists to their subordinates.

In order to rationalize all the sado-masochism necessary to produce one of our "self-made" captains of
industry, there developed a smoke screen about what
great sportsmen most of them were; how, after all, the
military and the corporation were just another kind of
"team"; and how the "players" had to do their jobs,
and the "coaches" had theirs. Thus Packard talks glow-
ingly about how the "dynamic executive" has "go-go-
go," is a "man of action," "works hard to beat last
year," "stays fit," and quotes an official to the effect
that execs "drive, drive, drive all the time." But, interestingly, our executive quarterback "keeps rivals off
balance, subordinates uncertain, superiors whom he
hopes to outflank unwary. He is much too wise to permit feelings of resentment of authority to color his behavior. Nor is our deft people-handler squeamish when
he feels he must get rid of a team player." Here we can
clearly see a celebration in sports mystifications—because they somehow sound more agreeable—of the
same sort of ambivalence to authority—hatred of authority, combined with rapt acceptance of it, and lack

of "squeamishness" about using it on others—which Wilhelm Reich in his book *The Mass Psychology of Fascism* describes as one of the most characteristic features of authoritarian character structure.[2]

Whether or not the militarized interiors of our monopoly corporations, presidential administrations, or our athletic programs attain the level of brutality of fascism, there is no doubt that they can be pretty sick places. Our organization men may learn some of their sado-masochism on the playing fields, but isn't it a little misleading, though more agreeable, to describe the kind of hatchetwork that goes on in climbing up the military or business pyramids as "good, clean American sport"?

[2] Indeed, the tendency to paint military or dictatorial activities in the colors of sports events is becoming quite generalized, leading to an Orwellian world in which—as we've seen—an Associated Press correspondent describes the war in Vietnam in the language of a baseball game. Or again, "taking the field in Cambodia" is used as a polite expression for an invasion. The artillery of "fighting inflation" by imposing mass unemployment is just "The Nation's Economic Game Plan." (*Life* magazine in August 1971 even appeared with a cover of President Nixon and Treasury Secretary Connally in football uniforms directing our "attack.") And the blockade of Haiphong is just "Operation Linebacker."

> For this great nation . . . to withdraw from
> the competition of the world, for the
> United States of America to quit trying to be
> No. 1, would be a very grave error . . .
> because once an individual or once a nation
> ceases to try to do its best to be No. 1,
> then that individual or that nation ceases
> to be a great individual or a great nation.
> Richard M. Nixon

6

Socialization for Production

A couple of years ago when I was a student in London, I happened to tune in to one of Britain's televised World Cup soccer matches. The announcer—decked out in his Union Jack tie—described the English team as "controlled," "disciplined," "composed," "well worked out," "competitive"; though one player, he added, was "a little too negative, should be more positive." With these plugs for competitiveness, discipline and positive thinking, he seemed to be giving us a scorecard of the supposedly desirable attributes for capitalism's well worked out, composed working class.

The mythology assumes that the Rules of the Game of life in capitalist society are perfectly neutral, so that success—whether in sport or civilian life—depends fun-

damentally on your attitude. If you follow the rules—
or play the game—compete hard, put out to make it,
and never give up, you can win the rat race. Of course
we all know that in sports, as in life, there can only be
a few winners—that is the way the game is set up. This
is the reason why the others must learn to be *good
losers,* accepting their defeats gracefully, always imag-
ining that we'll do better next time, but never questioning the Rules of the Game. If the system is to continue, the losers must be socialized both to *accept* their
position and to continue to play. In fact, both the
sports ethic and the Protestant ethic teach you that if
you lost the game, it was basically because you didn't
work hard enough. Vince Lombardi would say you had
an improper attitude. But you should be a "good
sport" about it. Everybody hates a "quitter." So keep
in training. Don't drop out. Wait for the "breaks." And
play the game.

Football, more than any other sport, has socialization
for elitism built right into its rules. The quarterback is
the "brain" of the team. He calls the signals and gives
the orders and the linemen have to protect him. He is
supposedly more valuable than they are. And he gets
a much higher salary. Typically he does not even go
through the same blocking and tackling practice drills
as the rest of the team, because he might get hurt. In
a game he is involved in less bruising body contact than
any other player, but if he does get hit, everyone is
worried about him. (Also he's almost always white.)
The offensive hierarchy's next rung is the backs and
ends. The linemen block for them—get their teeth
knocked out for them—but it is the backs and ends who
get the glory.

The power relations are indicated roughly by how
much each player handles the football. The quarterback takes the ball on every play from the center—
there are almost no black centers in the National Football League—and gives it to one or the other of the

backs or ends. Except for the center snap, the offensive
linemen are not allowed to touch the ball at all. On
defense it is more of the same. Here the key man is
the middle-linebacker. He makes the most tackles, usually calls the defensive signals, and is the man in the
middle. (Almost always he's white.) Next on the hierarchy are the outside linebackers, who, with very few
exceptions, in the NFL, are also white. Behind them
are the defensive backs—in the NFL, predominantly
black. And in front, the mammoths of the defensive
line—typically, huge and dumb.

In football as in industry generally, elitism is fos-
tered by proliferating specialization. Football has a
higher degree of division of labor and specialization
than any other American game. Not only are there different positions—as in baseball, too—but the skills necessary to play them are so different that different
specialists even come in different body sizes. And the
amount of specialization is increasing. Before the NCAA
introduced the free substitution rule, everyone had to
play both offense and defense. Even the glamor boy
quarterback. There could be no place-kicking specialist. No special punter. No suicide squad for kicks and
kick returns. With the introduction of free substitution
a decade ago all this changed. Some coaches even introduced whole squads of specialists. Paul Dietzel, the
head coach at Louisiana State and then Army, popularized a three-squad system. His top team—the guys
who started and could play either offense or defense
—he called, fittingly enough, "the white team." (They
must have loved this in Louisiana.) His offensive specialists, he called, again fittingly enough, "the go team."
(Presumably they had go-go-go.) The defensive specialists were "the Chinese bandits." (Why *Chinese*
bandits?) It was said that this system enabled every
player to identify with and feel pride in his unit, just
like in the army.

"I think football has come to look quite a bit like our

country does at certain times," ex-New York Jets All-Pro flanker George Sauer told Jack Scott. "I think the same powers that keep a football player pretty much locked in place throughout his whole career are the same kind of powers that would tend to keep black men, disadvantaged minorities, Mexican Americans, and Indians locked in place. The ideology of football's power structure is pretty much the same as that of the nation's power structure." (The interview is reprinted in *Intellectual Digest*, December 1971.)

He then went on to connect the ideology of football with the old social Darwinism ethic that a society is strengthened by a kind of social selection in which everyone competes against everyone else and the best come racing to the top. He pointed out that the sort of people who dug this "plutocratic, elitist, authoritarian ideology . . . were the people already up there on top with all the money." (The sort of people who own sports teams and insist on absolute respect, obedience, and discipline from their players.)

Not surprisingly, social Darwinism came into vogue in the last third of the nineteenth century, more or less at the same point in time when the rise of monopoly capital was making competition at the top of the social pyramid almost a thing of the past. Social Darwinism formed not only the perfect cloak for monopolistic rule at home, but also the perfect justification for racism and imperialism abroad. The general idea was that those races and classes that had successfully "competed" and made it to the top were obviously most "fit" to rule. The notion was extended to cover the "fitness" of men to rule over women. Darwin was drafted into the service of elitism, nationalism, racism, sexism, and the authoritarianness of the prevailing order generally. If you didn't like it, you were told to keep running, compete harder.

But under the rule of monopoly capital how much free competition really exists? And how fair is it? The

race of capitalist society is like a mile run in which some
of the competitors start with a three-quarter-mile lead.
In this "game" some players come into the competition
with a few million under their belts, while others get
their "training" in ghetto slums. These are indeed the
supposedly neutral Rules of the Game in a class
society. Although in sports and life success is supposed
to depend only on natural ability and hard drive, in
fact one side is forced to play with shackled legs.

But the world of sports mythology is a world where
poor boys *do* become millionaires. We read about it
every day. What we don't read is that for every one
who makes it to the top, there are thousands of athletes who don't, who maybe don't even make it into
the big leagues, but who keep chasing the elusive
brass ring of success till they drop exhausted. Recently,
the United Press circulated a story about Bruce Gardner who in 1960 had been voted the Most Valuable
College Baseball Player by the NCAA coaches. He had
run up the phenomenal intercollegiate record of forty
wins against only five losses. He had his heart set on a
big league pitching career. And coming out of school
he had been signed for a big bonus by the Los Angeles
Dodgers. However, after four years of disciplined work
up and down the Dodger farm system, he was uncon-
ditionally released. "He always thought he could make
it in the majors," said a close friend. "That's the one
thing he wanted."

Recently Gardner's body was found a short distance
from the pitching mound on the USC baseball field.
Near his body was his NCAA All-American plaque. In
one hand was his USC diploma. In the other hand was
a revolver. He had committed suicide. Aside from the
absolute finality of his end, Gardner's story was far
more typical of the sports rat race than all the success
stories we hear about. Not surprisingly, not too many
sportswriters were interested in it. It wasn't their kind

of news. Doubtless everyone would have said that Gardner had the wrong attitude.

But what's the right attitude? New York Rangers' hockey coach Emile Francis once remarked, "The good ones in this game are real thoroughbreds. They come to play every night. Money is important but not the motivating force, the thing that separates them from the average player. My guys belong in that category. They'll give out, won't loaf . . ."

The Toronto *Globe* magazine had an interview with the coach of that city's team in the Canadian Football League. Coach Leo Cahill told them that he considers the players his "friends." Until they get out of line. "Then I'll do what it takes right up to getting rid of them." He talked about the thing that makes (well-socialized) professionals what they are:

> That's down-in-the-dirt hard work and sweat and toughness and determination. That's the secret of their success, but some of these kids are not very smart. This is where class [?] prevails. This is when a guy understands that he is only as good as his next game and that he doesn't have many friends unless he's making a contribution.

The magazine points out that, even at gin rummy, the coach "competes fiercely," "never letting up," trying to "psyche out" his opponent, telling him he can't win—"playing to win, always to win." "I hate to lose," says the coach, "because I hate to lose. I made my mind up a long time ago that some guys are winners and some guys are losers. I'm a winner and I'm going to win . . ." He says, "Football coaches are a special breed." And all this is precisely the kind of elitism and hypercompetitiveness he teaches his players and fans: There are a few guys who make it to the top; they're the ones with "class"; they do it through "hard work and sweat and toughness and determination"; and they never let up because they're playing to win, win, win.

Players and fans are thus socialized for capitalist production. They are socialized to have the kind of acquisitive personalities the system demands. They are taught to want to run up their scores, to make the grade, get to the top of the heap, compete, drive, fight, fight, fight. "Hungry" players. "Money" players. Of course, they're only supposed to compete and fight against each other, never against the management. A ballplayer—or a worker—is taught to accept (without question!) the authority of his coaches and managers. His job is just to keep fit, keep plugging, keep improving his performance, stick to it, and know his place (or plays) on the sports or company team. He's supposed to be loyal to the team. (This often means—put out for, but don't knock, the management.) If he's learned all that, he is sometimes called "a coach's dream."

A recent article in the Toronto *Star* about the local CFL pro football team explained, "The players don't object to being robots, at least not openly. It wouldn't do any good anyway. [The coach's] decrees are not to be ignored. If the quarterback thinks he has a better idea, or knows a reason why the designated manoeuvre will fail, he's still wiser to do as he's told."

Dave Raimey, formerly an All-CFL back with the Winnipeg team, once remarked: "Here in Winnipeg, football players should be robots. They should do what they're told and then go home. We never have the slightest idea what our game plan is—I just go out, get in my stance, and go down the field on the first play . . . I think you should do what you're told to do [?], but you should also be convinced that what you're doing is right." Then he added, "Maybe I'm wrong. Maybe I *am* trying to be the coach." Naturally with attitudes like that, Raimey was promptly traded. (You can't have the workers telling the manager what to do.) It happens all the time. A guy will argue a little too long over his contract or not jump fast enough when his coach barks an order, or he might commit what

Jim Bouton calls the cardinal sin of questioning the coach, or he might be a black ballplayer that has white girl friends. Before you know it, word gets around that the guy's a "troublemaker." He lacks a "big league attitude." If he's still in the league after being traded once or twice, he quickly gets the message: Play "ball" our way or get out!

Many get thrown out. And owners have their own informal blacklists for cases like this. Former National Football League players Bernie Parrish, Freeman White, Walter Beach, and Johnny Sample testified about such blacklisting before a federal grand jury. (Beach had previously made a complaint about this to the Equal Employment Opportunities Commission.) Parrish had been trying to organize a players' association. As quarterback George Ratterman later put it, "In this league the quickest way to get a reputation as a troublemaker is to read your contract." The year before, Steve Wright, a 250-pound tackle for the New York Giants, was reportedly suspended for having an improper attitude. (The Giants' owner was well known to have a mania about clean language and church attendance. He even used to bring a priest into the locker room before every home game to lead everyone in prayers.) Just before the following season the Giants' brass dropped Wright completely. He eventually caught on with another team.

The owners have any number of tactics they can use on unruly serfs—fines, benching, suspensions, a trip to the minors, unconditional release, and, if all that fails, the blacklist. For example, when Jim Bouton refused to sign his contract with the Yankees one year, General Manager Ralph Houk threatened to fine him a hundred dollars for every day he was out of spring training, where the rule was only signed players could attend. (It reminds you of the old days at the turn of the century when it was sometimes the practice to fine unions for every day they went on strike.) So common was the

fining of NHL hockey players by their owners that even
the Rea Commission on Canadian Sports took issue with
such arbitrary practices. It is as if your boss could sum-
marily fine you any time he feels like it. In Bouton's
case, after his salary squabble with the management,
he was, despite his previous excellent pitching record,
suddenly dropped from the starting rotation, and soon
found himself in the minors. When he wrote a mildly
irreverent book on baseball, he was immediately ordered into the commissioner's office. The official attitude toward what was called "knocking the game," he
later recalled, was that (as the commissioner put it)
if you were selling cars, you shouldn't be telling people about their lousy transmissions. And so, too, with
America's National Pastime.

Another case was Jim Brosnan. In the early sixties
he wrote two books (even more harmless than Bouton's) about the pomposity of certain baseball managers and the wild machinations of the front-office
brass. So in 1962 he was shipped from the Cincinnati
Reds to the Chicago White Sox. With the Sox he was
made into a relief pitcher and had a so-so season, but
with a very good—2.84—earned run average. He was
offered a contract with a 20 per cent salary cut—and
with the added stipulation that he do no further writing. (It was pointed out that paragraph 3(c) of the
uniform baseball contract—titled "LOYALTY"—*forbids
players from saying or writing anything "without written consent of the Club."*) When he refused these conditions, he was put on waivers. No one picked him up.
As a general point, the technique of putting a player
you want blackballed out on waivers, after first being
assured by the other owners that no one will pick him
up, is becoming quite a standard way to wreck a guy's
career. This is what Carl Furillo, the old Dodger right
fielder claims happened to him. Parrish, Beach, and
Sample claim they got this treatment, too.

Then there was the story of All-NHL defenseman

Doug Harvey's efforts to form a pro hockey players' association. Originally, the overt issue there—as in all other big league sports—was whether the players would get a pension fund. The owners were not enthusiastic. "They didn't want players to get together," says Doug Harvey. "They didn't want them talking to each other." Who knows, they might have started comparing notes about salaries, working conditions; you couldn't have that. Such is the fierce level of competition inculcated in pro hockey that Harvey later admitted that, "the hardest thing I ever had to do in hockey" was associate with a member of an opposing team—in this case, discussing the pension plan with Ted Lindsay of the Detroit Red Wings. Gradually, and with incredible difficulty the players began to get their association together:

> Unfortunately, it never got off the ground and some of the leaders, including Lindsay, got themselves into a lot of trouble with management. I know that Jack Adams, the Detroit manager, was angry with Lindsay and wound up sending him to the then lowly Chicago Black Hawks as punishment. Harvey asked me to join the association . . . I was sure that if I did . . . I would have been in even more hot water, particularly with Frank Selke [the Montreal boss]. He didn't want me to have any part of the union. (Rocket Richard in Stan Fischler's book, *The Flying Frenchmen*.)

Suddenly the axe started falling in all directions. Montreal militant Bert Olmstead was traded to Toronto, and Dollard St. Laurent went to Chicago. Later Donnie Marshall and Jacques Plante were shipped out. At Toronto, association leader Dick Duff was sent packing. Bill Gadsby was switched from Chicago to New York, and Fern Flaman left Boston. (A similar purge of player reps occurred a couple of years ago following the baseball players' strike. Joe Torre, perhaps the top player in baseball, was shipped from Atlanta to St. Louis; Clete Boyer ended up in the minors; and so on.) Doug Harvey nevertheless seemed fairly secure in Montreal—after all, he was in the process of winning the Norris trophy as the league's top defenseman for the sixth time. He was team captain, had the highest seniority on the club, and the management had even asked him if he was interested in coaching. During the off season he was asked to go on a tour out West to promote beer for Montreal's beer baron ownership (i.e., Molsons). When he returned he found his contract had been sold to New York.

The connection between sports, competition and elitism is no accident. Looking back through history we can see that success in battle or blood sports provided the first measure of status, indeed one of the first concepts of valuation. (Our word "wage" originates from the same root as "gage," the symbol of agonistic challenge.) At first the best warriors became the rulers. Back in those ancient and medieval days, prowess in battle sport had a very clear import for the community. Its continued existence might depend on how well the young men could fight. Later, with the rise of a hereditary royalty, the most valorous blood-sportsmen would be accorded special prizes and praise, but no special political privilege. Our athletic "heroes" fare even worse. Their status has become more and more just a ritualized—and increasingly empty—crumb. We regard them as super-animals, heroes of the moment, or just jocks. One reason is that just being an athlete is no longer a direct measure of any socially necessary skill. Yesterday's heroes become tomorrow's has-beens. While the game lasts, sports success still confers a kind of status. We have all seen hot-shot fraternities competing against one another for the biggest jocks on campus. But these days frats are dying even faster than jockery. Yet, ironically, swelling college enrollment has, in numerical terms, made the small group of varsity sportsmen more of an elite than ever before. They think of themselves as the guys who have "made it."

In a way they have. But only because "our" intercollegiate and professional sports are constructed in such a way that a small elite plays while the vast majority watches. The money and resources that might have been put into intramural sports in which everyone could be a "player" has, instead, been put into sports for an elite, because elite games are more marketable. (And, in capitalist society, so is elitism.) We saw earlier how, historically, there was nothing "natural" and "inevitable" about this. Historically, the split between the field and the stands developed at the same time as the split between the factory managers controlling production and the workers performing their fragmented, bureaucratized tasks on the assembly lines. (In *Soul on Ice* Cleaver speaks of the split between "omnipotent administrators" and "supermasculine menials.") Both the "fan" and the "unskilled" (or "specialized") worker had to be created. In practice both the fans and the players are menials. Those in the stands are encouraged to identify with the "supermasculine" menials on the field—an elite, but only in respect of bodily prowess, an elite socialized to split their minds from their bodies and to do what they're told:

> They don't really allow the athlete to be a human being. On one hand he is supposed to be more human and on the other he is supposed to be less human. On one hand he is superman and he is a jock and he is a body, and on the other hand he is expected to be pretty much compliant with traditional authority—being told what to do. I would never say that athletes are exactly like slaves were, but there is something about organized athletics that treats an athlete somewhat as a slave. The attitude still exists that we are a body and that we are property and we

do the heavy work while the thinkers are out doing
something else . . . The way football is structured
today, being an athlete is like being kept in perpetual
or prolonged adolescence. (All-Pro George Sauer,
op. cit.)

Sauer also hit all the mumbo-jumbo about how sports
programs develop an elite of self-disciplined and responsible adults. He said that the college and professional coaches know damn well they have never given
their jocks a chance to become responsible or self-
disciplined. Even in the pros, they tell them when to
turn the lights off, when to go to bed, when to wake
up, when to eat, what to eat, ad nauseum. Sauer compared it to living in a boys camp, and noted the same
people who are telling everyone how self-disciplined,
mature, and responsible this is making them are really
keeping the jocks in "an adolescent stage." The Jets'
flanker had more freedom in high school than he did
in the pros—at least in high school he never had to go
through pre-season bed checks. But "by the time you
get to the pros they know that the whole system has
kept you being too much of a child to allow you any
freedom."

Despite all the smooth smoke screens about how college sports produce "well-rounded men," today's college athletes are little more than extremely poorly paid
athletic workers. And despite all its pretended concern
for "academic" values and that old aristocratic chestnut
"amateurism," the NCAA's regulations about recruiting
and scholarships are little more than monopolistic
agreements in restraint of trade designed to keep down
the salaries of these workers. What sort of "education"
does the average college scholarship athlete really get?
Assuming he actually gets a degree, how much real
knowledge goes with it? And what sort of treatment
from his coaches has he had to put up with along the
way? The athletes themselves are asking these ques-

tions. Even Steve Owens, while he was in the course of winning college football's Heisman Trophy in 1969, told a reporter for *Sport* magazine, "In high school the game was almost entirely fun. Here it's a business.[1] We're supposed to fill that stadium with 60,000 fans and win . . . I still love the game, but there's so much pressure, sometimes it makes me wonder." (*Sport*, November 1969, p. 94.) Now that he is in the (openly) professional ranks, it must be even worse. Frank Champi, Harvard's star quarterback who decided he'd had enough after the second game of the 1969 season, said he had quit because football was ". . . too mechanized. It doesn't allow for the human being . . . We're like pieces of machinery . . . The whole concept of machine sports was just stopping me." (*Sport*, December 1969, p. 4.) The next year Fred Abbott, a sophomore linebacker at Florida billed as a potential All-America, walked off the team, saying, "The game has been exploited. I felt like a machine. The coaches

[1] A 1969 survey by the University of Missouri showed the fifty or so schools with major intercollegiate football programs spending an average of almost $670,000 on them, and around $1,300,000 on their athletic programs as a whole. Jack Scott has pointed out that with financial investments of this size, the stakes involved have become so enormous that "college football programs are now run like industrial corporations," complete with organization-man athletic administrators. In fact, as early as 1951, David Reisman and Reuel Denny pointed out, "the game is now a co-operative enterprise in which mistakes are too costly—to the head coach, the budget, even the college itself—to be left to individual initiative." A 1970 article in *Sport* magazine by Dave Wolf found that the University of Texas was spending around $50,000 a year just on athletic recruitment. As an example of what this money ultimately goes for, it might be worth pointing out that when Ohio State's football record dropped from 7–2 to 4–5 between 1965 and 1966, alumni contributions dropped by over 40 per cent, costing the school about $500,000.

called the shots and we just moved around. The game has evolved into a business, but with the pretext that it is a game. Coaches stress that winning is everything, but sportsmanship has been taken out of it." (Neil Amdur, *The Fifth Down*, New York: Coward, McCann & Geoghegan, 1971, pp. 60–61.) He later rejoined the team, but became one of a group of athletes including All-America pass receiver Carlos Alvarez to form their own union. Abbott's teammate, quarterback John Reaves (who had been the No. 1 passer in the country the preceding year) said he felt "like a robot." (St. Petersburg *Times*, September 19, 1970, p. 10.)

How could they make these statements? It isn't easy. In evaluating the successes and failures of the so-called "jock liberation movement," we have to keep in mind just what these players are up against. Not just in terms of authoritarian athletic institutions, but in terms of the relative isolation, narrowed world view, and distorted self-identities imposed on the athletes themselves. Not just by one coach. But usually by their whole athletic upbringing. From the first time our aspiring athlete made it to his first schoolboy or little league team, he had to keep his hair "neatly trimmed," possibly even in an Army crew-cut. Already he was being set aside, made to *look different* from other kids. More than likely all of his friends would tend to be fellow athletes or athletic boosters. If he was good at the game, his girl friend may even have been a cheerleader. By the time he was in college, he may have been living in a separate athletic dormitory, eating his meals separately, certainly taking separate (and, almost always, inferior) courses from the other students, possibly even going to separate parties or hanging about with a separate jock-set (most campuses have "jock" fraternities). In short, by the time he makes it to the first team of the college varsity, he is likely to be totally locked into the narrow circle of the jock world and the jock mentality, for which he was preselected. (An innovation in the selection process of late is the use of psychological testing to help choose those potential athletes who show most evidence of hypercompetitiveness, aggressiveness, and the need to fight, fight, fight to win, win, win.) Intellectually, the varsity or professional athlete is likely to have been held back—more or less deliberately retarded—so as to be more fully exploited as an athletic commodity. At the big-time universities, practice sessions are apt to be so long and so frequent the athletes literally don't have time for their courses. Lacking any intellectual background—even that which comes from having broad student friendships and involvements—the varsity or pro athlete literally cannot imagine doing anything that would bring him the same social rewards and prestige as sports, temporary as that prestige may be. *His whole self-identity is athletics.*

Even so, many have rebelled. But it is difficult. And those that do rebel are usually so appalled by what they see that they seldom wait around for an authoritarian coach to boot them off the team. They just quit. The odd pro footballer who does this—in George Sauer's case throwing up a $45,000-a-year contract—gets big publicity. But thousands of high school and college athletes have done the same. This is certainly one of the main tragedies of today's militarized, commercialized sports: They have been so brutalized by the society around them that an athlete who really enjoys sports and wants to be something more than a jock-machine finds that there is literally no place for him. Unless, of course, he gets together with other athletes to change things.

There are those, of course, apparently content to be athletic robots. Or at least too weak to try to be anything more satisfying. The big jocks—brutalized by their coaches, exploited by their teams, put through their paces like toy soldiers—have been permitted to "make it" to the top of a mythical dreamworld in which they can play Superman. Back in the real world, most take orders like good little tots. They have to. The labor market structure of their industry absolutely requires it (unless the players organize). No doubt all capitalists would like workers who are absolutely obedient, absolutely loyal to the company team, constantly striving to stay in shape, put out, improve their productivity, beat last year's figures, and so on. But all capitalists are not in the enviable position of professional sports owners (or even college coaches) of having perhaps as many as two score candidates for every job (though in practice they wouldn't bother to "draft" that many). Candidates who have no place else to go if the boss says their attitude is bad.

So the labor market is structured in that elitist pyramidal fashion that keeps the kids hustling harder and harder for a smaller and smaller number of places all the way up the pyramid to the pros at the top. This structure puts the sports owners and their managers in a stronger position to dictate the values of their subordinates than capitalists in virtually any other industry, provided, of course, the athletes remain unorganized. The only thing comparable is the pyramidal structure that screens out top management in the large corporations. There, too, the victims are totally unorganized. And there too—as Vance Packard shows in *The Pyramid Climbers*—the level of brutality and emphasis on having absolutely correct bourgeois attitudes is simply incredible. Because of this bottom-heavy labor market— with a mammoth reserve army of labor always in the wings—elitist sports serves as an ideological generator for the most neanderthal values of hypercompetitive, authoritarian, jungle capitalism.

But *why* do boys subject themselves to the brutality of competing, *in order* to "make it" in elitist sports? Bernie Parrish concludes his excellent inquiry into pro football *They Call It a Game* (p. 293) with the remark that players "feel part of something big and important, and that outweighs logic . . . They're swept up in its

exaggerated importance . . . TV makes it glamorous
. . . Every action and reaction is subject to detailed
analysis by the news media. Public awareness of the
sport is acute . . . The aura is intoxicating; for players,
it is absolutely stupefying. They will endure practically
anything to be part of the team." Nor is this an accident. Precisely because elitist sports are such a good
ideological generator for the most authoritarian and
competition-minded values of authoritarian capitalism,
it has received constant backing and pushing over the
years from the military, big business, and organized
religion.

From the viewpoint of the owners, the small elite of
top jocks does yeoman service. Not only do they help
socialize the working class to the elitism that is so essential in keeping them divided one from the other,
but they are also the perfect pseudo elite for the
workers to identify with—a beefsteak pseudo elite of
brawn not brain, myth without power, and one completely under the thumb of the real bosses. So we learn
our phony elitism.

Is the competitiveness taught by the sports establishment any less phony? We've already seen how the competitiveness is supposed to be directed only at the other
workers, not at the management. The origin of all the
competitiveness for starting places on varsity and pro
teams is that same elitist split between players and
fans. It is not necessary. The money now spent on
varsity teams and intercollegiate sports, for example,
could be spent on intramural sports aimed at making
everyone a player. If everyone was out playing they
would have much less time to be fans. And if they had
fulfilling, creative jobs, they wouldn't need to look for
the pseudo satisfactions of being fans.

The competitiveness between opposing teams is also
part of a pseudo world. What difference does it really
make who wins and who loses in sports? Jake Gaudaur,

Commissioner of the Canadian Football League, once perceptively remarked, "It matters not whether you win or you lose, just as long as the fans aren't sure in advance which it's going to be." (The *Financial Post,* November 28, 1970.) He perhaps should have added —"and just as long as the fans think that it's important." The question has been fairly thoroughly analyzed by my close friend Bob Kellermann:

> One can say that the relationship between producers (players) is really *not* one of competition between teams but rather they co-operate to produce a product (commodity) just as in other capitalist enterprises. However, here, unlike elsewhere, the product itself is the "spectacle-of-competition." Evidence that players consciously or unconsciously come to know this lies in the fact that there is a strong tendency to "fix" the game, i.e., produce the "appearance" of competition while at the same time actually co-operating. [Leonard Shecter gives scores of examples of this in his book *The Jocks.*] The "spectacle of competition" is, after all, only a spectacle, and its social function is served as long as the consumers (fans) believe there is competition. This is obvious in wrestling matches, where only particularly ignorant people believe in the appearance. The reality of fixed matches remains hidden to them. Similarly in horse-racing. (Only here almost all the bettors assume the thing is fixed, and try to figure out the pattern of fixes.)
>
> Perhaps the best proof of how the spectacle-of-competition is more important than whether there is real competition was the recent computer world championship of boxing. Here there was *no* fight at all, only the coming together of images, ghosts. Yet millions actually believed in the reality of the Marciano-Ali competition (and probably sat in their seats cheering).

The "winning" of the spectacle of competition is in fact the *least* important part of this social process, for it is the spectacle itself which is socially significant. Here we see that the reality is the exact opposite of the appearance, which in men's consciousness is expressed in the belief that winning is the only thing that counts. But obviously this winning is only important within the extremely narrow confines of the "rules of the game," which in these contests are, after all, only the rules of a *game* (an illusion). The reality is that there *must be both* a winner and a *loser* in order for the spectacle-of-competition to have any meaning. So that in *social* terms the losers are just as essential to the spectacle as the winners.

This becomes much clearer when one sees the spectacle of competition through the eyes of those who *own* and *sell* this product and who employ the workers (players) who produce it. What they want to see is a "good show." Who wins or loses is almost irrelevant, since the profits depend on the appearance of "good competition," not on who wins the game. This is obvious when one man owns both teams. (We've already seen that James Norris not long ago owned three teams in the National Hockey League.) But it is just as true when there are different owners who run one league together. After all, everyone knows that the owner of a losing team benefits from the appearance of a winning team at *his* arena where he collects the profits. And in the event that one team is too weak (i.e., cannot provide a marketable commodity when combined with another team in the spectacle) the other teams' owners will try to strengthen the losing team, which is a loser for *all* the owners in terms of profits. The strengthening of losers in order to ensure the spectacle-of-competition, which ensures profits, is institutionalized in the *draft*, a process whereby the weakest teams—their compet-

itive weakness on the field is almost certainly to be
reflected at the box office—are allowed first choice of
the new players. (Moreover, in the Canadian Football League, for example, the owners actually have
a gate equalization pot, whereby those "losers" who
attract fewest fans are paid receipts from the
"winners.")

The real competition, which is not just appearance
is (i) the competition between producers to make
the same team, (ii) the competition between owners of opposing leagues [although even here there is
very strong evidence that although owners in opposing leagues compete for rookies, they usually have
a "truce" on veterans]. In the latter case we see the
problem which capitalism inevitably faces—satura-
tion of markets. There are only so many commodities
(spectacles-of-competition) which a particular market of consumers (fans) can absorb. This can result
in owners of these spectacles competing to sell their
products since not all will be able to dispose of them.
Thus, when the AFL first started, the NFL owners
opposed it bitterly because they saw it as a threat
to their profits, though they tried to disguise their
real interest by alluding to the quality of football,
etc. The AFL, being new in the market, had to break
the "brand loyalty" of the NFL consumers and therefore sold their tickets (product) at a lower price.
Of course they also tried to tap new customers by
going to different cities if possible. But TV makes
the market almost nationwide so competition was
inevitable.

Of course once their product caught on they
raised their prices, and the consumers who benefited
from this short [untypical in the stage of monopoly
capitalism] bout of competition were once again fac-
ing monopoly rip-off prices. This brief bit of competition also helped the producers (i.e., players).
While it lasted the AFL capitalists were forced to

pay higher salaries in order to sign rookies to produce the same quality spectacle-of-competition and prevent them from going to the NFL. So there was a price war for a short period in which some producers and consumers were the beneficiaries.

If the NFL had had the power to keep the AFL out of business, and thereby protect their right to exploit the market as a monopolist, they would have done so. But the AFL was able to make it a battle. Therefore, like all good capitalists, the owners of both leagues realized that their competition was only benefiting the consumers and the producers, and unlike the spectacles they sell, they decided they would *both* be winners. Thus, in contrast to the ideology they perpetrate, in true monopolist fashion they decided to merge. This way they could agree to share the market, raise their prices together and ensure the continued rip-off of the consumers (fans). They could also stop the situation which put the producers (players) in a stronger bargaining position. When the two leagues were competing the players could in theory play one off against the other and get slightly better salaries. But once the leagues merged the players were again faced with only one possible employer, since they would now all be subject to the same draft and same monopoly.

It is important to see that in their behavior as capitalists in the monopoly stage of capitalism, these owners *avoid* competition with each other at all costs while, at the same time, they sell a product whose main ideological function is to perpetrate the belief in competition.

It might be added that whenever the players suggest that the reserve or option clauses that bind them to indentured servitude for one owner be discarded, the owners bashfully retreat behind the veil of their pretended competition and claim that this would mean

that the richest team would sign all the best players.
At the stage of monopoly capitalism, this is simply
nonsense. If there was any danger of this happening,
the owners would simply collude to stop it. They could,
for example, pass a statute preventing any given team
from signing more than a certain number of players
from other teams each year. Because General Motors
is richer than Chrysler does not mean that they sign
all the best engineers. They are all in the game together.

Organized team sport is really becoming the passive
robot production of the assembly line, and increasingly
of the now proletarianized white collar jobs as well. In
Veblen's day, opiates like sports, betting, and religion
may have been enough to provide the drugged workers
for drugged production. In our own time, as the legitimacy of the system has eroded further, as the gap between "democratic" mythology and authoritarian reality becomes more and more painful, the functioning of
the system from one moment to another requires *real
drugs.* And it requires them in great quantities. *Ramparts* magazine has produced much evidence to support the contention that the world's leading drug dealer
is the Central Intelligence Agency. In New York the
Knapp Commission found much evidence that the leading drug dealers in New York, along with and in part-
nership with organized crime, were the members of
the New York City Police Department. Bernie Parrish,
Dave Meggyesy, Chip Oliver, and Jack Scott have produced much evidence in their books to prove that
the biggest drug dealers in the sports world are none
other than the team trainers. "Greenies are pep pills
—dextroamphetamine sulfate," writes Jim Bouton, "and
a lot of baseball players couldn't function without
them." (*Ball Four*, New York: Dell Books, 1971, p.
80.) Writes Chip Oliver, "If Pete Rozelle, the commissioner of the National Football League, put a lock

on the pill bottle, half the players would fall asleep in
the third quarter . . . many professional players
couldn't have made a move without them." (*High For
the Game*, p. 44.) At first they might just take them
before a big game. Then it was before every game.
Then they had to take them just to practice. "As the
players get older," he says, "they forget about how to
get energy naturally and start getting it from ampheta-
mine pep pills they call rat turds." (Ibid., p. 65.) After
the game they are so high, they have to be tranquilized
to get their eyeballs back in their heads—to even get a
night's sleep. Ken Gray filed a $3.5 million lawsuit
against the St. Louis Cardinals, their team physician,
and their trainer charging he was administered "potent,
illegal, and dangerous drugs . . . so that he would perform more violently." The drugs were dextroamphetamine sulfate, chlorpromazine hydrochloride, and so-
dium pentobarbital. Gray's suit alleges they were given
to him "deceptively and without consent either expressed or implied," and as a result he sustained "injuries, nervousness, restlessness, and sleeplessness,
severe and persistent headache, and his general health
and body integrity were diminished." A similar $1¼
million medical suit was filed by defensive lineman
Houston Ridge against the San Diego Chargers.

In June and July 1969 Bill Gilbert wrote a three-part
special for *Sports Illustrated* exposing the incredibly
widespread use of drugs in American sports. On October 20, 1970 a California State Legislative Subcommittee on Drug Abuse and Alcoholism held a special hearing on drug abuse in athletics. The chairman of the
subcommittee pointed out that in our regulations
against drug use in horse racing we do at least seem to
be showing due regard for the health of the animals.
"I believe it is incumbent upon us, at this hearing today,"
he said, "to do no less for human competitors." (Nevertheless, after pressure from various pro $port$ czars
was applied, no further hearings or legislation were

initiated.) Mike Mohler, a football player at Berkeley, interviewed every player on the California team and found that 48 per cent of them used speed. Twenty-eight per cent admitted they used anabolic steroids, the weight-producing drugs that have also been known to produce atrophy of the testicles, cancer of the prostate, and sterility. Mohler told Jack Scott he had reason to believe that such drug use was even more common at other big West Coast schools than at Berkeley.

Paul Lowe, the running back with the San Diego Chargers testified, "We had to take them [anabolic steroids] at lunch time. He [the trainer] would put them on a little saucer and prescribed for us to take them and if not he would suggest there might be a fine." (Scott, op. cit., pp. 144–45.) Amphetamines were also supplied in abundance. "The trainer of the Cardinals," remarked Dave Meggyesy, (pp. 91, 98, 99) "had what amounted to a drugstore down in his training room. The drug cabinets were open and could be used by any of the players . . . They extensively used cortisone, xylocaine, and novocain to shoot injured ballplayers up before the game . . ." This might be the only way they could keep playing, keep producing, but how many other injuries did it lead to along the way? Bernie Parrish (op. cit., pp. 5, 69, 74) admitted that his general practice was to dose himself with 70 milligrams of Dexedrine before every game. "I never played another game," wrote Parrish after he first learned of pep pills in college, "in my college or professional career without taking either Dexedrine or Benzedrine." He and Ross Fichtner of the Browns had very serious reactions after mixing a muscle-relaxing drug and beer. Fichtner had convulsions and Parrish passed out (for four hours) while at the wheel of his car. "The laws say that you cannot take such powerful drugs unless they are prescribed by a physician," he says. "Yet they were made available to us by our trainer, as was the case on most other professional teams." The latest joke making the rounds of professional sports is that it's not players and coaches who win championships, but pharmacists! In these militarized times, the sportscasters usually refer to the platoon that covers kick-offs and punts as the "bomb squad." The players, much more to the point, call it the "bennies squad."

Jack Scott (op. cit., pp. 148, 150) says that when he was covering the 1968 Olympics, the discussions among the U. S. track and field men were not about whether it was right or healthy to take drugs, but which drugs were most effective and which could you get away with. At the 1960 Olympics, Danish cyclist Knud Jensen collapsed and *died* after his race. It was established that he had taken Ronicol, a blood-vessel dilating drug. Scott says, "It is widely recognized in track and field circles that it is next to impossible to get to the top in most weight events and the decathlon without the use of these drugs since most of the top athletes are using them." For example, anabolic steroids have been used to put twenty, thirty, even sixty pounds of added plastic muscle on a jock's frame. (These drugs were developed, after all, to fatten up prize cattle!) But in many cases they have the embarrassing side effect of shrinking the testes. So the tendency seems to be toward the production of *plastic Supermen with no balls.* In the case of pep pills, what starts out as an added edge to help jocks win championships, produce more, becomes in the end a necessity just to get them to function at all.

There is nothing unique about this in America. One medical study I saw estimated that the average American consumes about a dozen pills per day. In many districts tranquilizers are even being given to tiny school children, to keep them nicely quiet and functioning. We are rapidly reaching the point where the whole society is patched together with drugs and could not function without them. In fact, that point may already have been passed. It's not surprising that the sports world finds itself in the same bag. But the NCAA and the NFL issuing solemn warnings against drugs on their telecasts each week is like the Mafia issuing warnings against crime. The system and its victims cannot function without drugs, and pretty soon they will not be able to function with them.

> Thus production creates not only an object for an individual, but also an individual for the object.
>
> Marx

7

Socialization for Consumption

I can still remember playing punchball with the kids in my elementary school in New York. The games were fairly relaxed affairs, chosen up on the spur of the moment. Winning took second place to enjoyment. It was fun. And if you asked me a couple of days later, "who hit what?" I probably couldn't have told you. It was just another part of childhood, along with tag, marbles, and hopscotch.

When I entered junior high school all this changed. Suddenly everyone was playing basketball. If you couldn't play, you were a "sissy," and that was that. The fight for status was on. Competitive sports was the battleground. The school authorities did everything they could to push it. Every class had its own team,

which, like miniature nations, would contest for laurels
against the other classes. There was even an All-Star
Game. To cap it all the school sponsored an "Athlete
of the Year" award. Inter-personal rivalries became
fierce. Fist fights broke out on the courts all the time.
And the kids were cock-fighting about more than scoring hoops.

I joined the rat race. I remember spending incredibly
long hours on the courts practicing. Every kid in the
neighborhood was doing the same—or wanted to. It was
only in my middle twenties, when I came across Leonard Koppett's book on the National Basketball Association, that I started wondering about what all the time
I'd spent on sports had gone for. This neighborhood
mania for basketball which had done so much to distort
the values and lives of so many people was, in fact,
something artificially created by the owners of professional basketball teams in order to supply themselves
with a booming market in players and fans. The same
thing had happened in every other sport. Owners were
pushing their product into the brains of kids via the
media, the schools, toy balls in crackerjacks boxes, trading cards, ads on cereal boxes, billboards, bank windows, posters, pennants, little leagues.

And in the hypercompetitive, status-oriented jungle
being created by monopoly capitalism, in which work
is at best almost meaningless and play the best available escape, the pitch for basketball went over big. This
is not to say that owners single-handedly created the
market for these sports. In a society of fragmented and
uncreative work, most people are particularly pleased
to exercise their creative faculties in new games. After
all, for most people it is their only creative outlet. (This
also explains in part the rise of conspicuous consumption, and particularly the recent rise in the conspicuous
consumption of sex. It may not be much of a game, but
for many it's the only game in town.) And in a society
without sufficient athletic facilities for everyone to play,

it is very likely that most people will end up as spectators of other people's play.

Successive generations of sports owners have cashed
in on this phenomenon in our society. The manufacture
and sale of mass pro-basketball watching was only
one of their many manipulative achievements. Perhaps
I was able to see it easiest with this sport because the
promotional boom for basketball was just picking up
steam in the early fifties. It had not been around long
enough for us to imagine that it always was there, and
always would be.

Today, the minds of children are still being retooled
so that owners and nations can reap profits and glory.
"We bubble the kids in at the broad base of the
pyramid," says an official of an Ontario Ski Association
for children ages seven and up, "and squirt gold medals
through the top. Too many people are afraid of competition. We teach the youngsters how to enjoy it." An
article in the Toronto *Telegram* claims this is all part
of a "long-range development plan that is already paying dividends" in national and international competition, because it's got "organizational and financial support." And, "as the talent rises to the top," the best kids
get "bumped up" to a Canadian National Training
Squad to act as stand-bys for future Olympics. The
others presumably make good ski fans. This was only a
recent example. More generally, R. E. Snyder of the
National Sporting Goods Association has pointed out
(in his pamphlet *The Sporting Goods Market Outlook
is . . . GREAT!*, Chicago: NSGA, 1968) that the main
factor in the present high development of the sporting goods market has been "the promotion and wide
scale development of organized play programs of all
kinds for youngsters, under institutional and government sponsorship, not to mention the proliferation of
competitive sports programs for industrial workers in
many fields." He adds, "the United States has long
since been transformed from a nation of sitters into a

nation of hitters. They hit balls, they hit baskets, they hit targets, they hit pucks, they hit surfboards, they hit water, they hit the dirt, they hit the snow, they hit the throttle and a-racing they go . . . and hitting the bottle isn't exactly taboo, either." Also, "hitters double in brass as sitters," so they help the industry, "not only as purchasers of its products but also as supporters of its spectator sports extravaganzas."

And all the hitting is manipulated from the top by the people skimming off the profits. The National Hockey League, for example, gets essentially all its players from north of the border. So when a government commission in Ottawa set up Hockey Canada to encourage growth of that "sport," representatives from the three Canadian NHL teams were naturally put on the board of directors. And the Canadian Amateur Hockey Association (which supplies essentially all the pro hockey players) gets its biggest charity grant from —guess where—the NHL. (Similarly, the Canadian Amateur Football Association gets its biggest grant from the Canadian Football League.) Take baseball. The minor leagues and little league teams have been kept in business with generous grants from the Major Leagues and baseball business interests. And since there is no developed system of minor league basketball and football, the colleges, in effect, provide the pros with their farm system. It is all part of an unwritten deal whereby the colleges are allowed to skim off some of the profits in exchange for building up the "sport," and providing pro owners with an overcrowded (and hence, cheap) player market and lots of future fans. Even the Amateur Athletic Association is not far behind:

> Years ago, the AAU established its Junior Olympics [involving, he said, *millions* of boys and girls] to *create* interest by American youth in the Olympic sports, to encourage participation in Amateur Athletics . . . and, *above all, to create a love for com-*

petition. Today, it is competition in athletics—tomorrow, it will be competition in the business world. (AAU President, David A. Matlin, *Amateur Athlete,* Vol. 39, No. 7, p. 7, my emphases.)

We have previously seen how the fragmented and bureaucratized nature of social relations in capitalist production, together with the workers' increased leisure and higher-than-subsistence wages, laid the material basis for the development in the last third of the nineteenth century of an entertainment industry and of hyperconsumption generally. The sports industry as the vanguard of the new "entertainment" phenomena was also an extremely useful and powerful device for selling all the later forms of mass entertainment from popular newspapers to television. Along with this it sold its "fans" on the "entertainment" way of thinking, by which people are transformed into a passive "audience" for those few specialist "performers" from whom they expect diversion and escape. The entertainment way of thinking, which was to be epitomized in the rise of the "spectator" (a new form of "mass consumer") in what was to become "spectator sport," *accepted* the barrenness of work under capitalism and looked only for new consumption opiates to help forget about it. It held that work was unimportant. The important thing was diversion. "Did you see the game last week?" one aspiring spectator might ask another in the latter decades of the nineteenth century. And the two could then go on to have a conversation about events of no real importance whatever.

Suddenly baseball (in England, soccer) goings-on had become something to know about, something guys who didn't even know one another could have in common, talk about. Sartre once pointed out that most people read newspapers, not to get news, but to gain community. To gain the collective reinforcement of their values that comes with reading again and again and again that everybody else (a few crackpots excepted) is doing more or less the same things, thinks the same things are important, and that—whatever private doubts we might have about it, whatever gnawing dissatisfactions we might be nursing in our brains (or loins)—*this* Way of Life is the only possibility, and fairy-tale princesses apart, there is no alternative. He might just as well have been talking about the reasons for going to baseball games. (Or, indeed, about all forms of popular entertainment.) The activity itself might have been completely idiotic—and people were not so stupid that they didn't know this, but once the promotional bandwagon got rolling, baseball games became something every American male could go to, every American male could talk about with the boys (even his boss!) and use to make a few more friends, feel a little less lonely. (In a period when the rising mass production monopolies were relegating vast numbers of people to the fragmentation, monotony, and alienation of the assembly line, this was no small thing.) And so, since this mass moronization seemed harmless enough—in fact, just what assembly line work demands!—capitalists were not unhappy when their advertising maestros in the press dubbed baseball "America's National Pastime," soccer was lauded as "essential to British Society," and ice hockey became "Canada's National Religion." The "fan" had been born, and through its newspapers, capitalism was giving him its nod of approval. (All that was missing was a Blue Ribbon from the brewers—and darned if someone didn't come up with that, too. Baseball and beer.)

Sports watching is still one of the most powerful socializers for the habit of passive consumption around. For example, consider the similarities between the fan, the consumer, the voter, and the student. All have learned to take in, more or less passively, a product assembled by other people—be it a sports spectacle, a consumer good, a candidate or preprocessed particles of knowledge. They are all supposed to accept the guidance on how to consume of their reigning expert—be he the sportscaster, the fashion or "modern living" columnist, the political correspondent, or the professor. And all four "games" have their statistics and stars of spectacle—whether they be called sports superstars, movie stars, presidents, or professorial stars like Arthur Schlesinger, Jr. ("If all the record books disappeared tomorrow," says Bill Beeck in *The Hustler's Handbook*, "baseball would disappear with them.")

In all of these spheres we can see that it is not a case of people demanding certain products, for despite the myths of "consumer sovereignty" or "democracy," the people in capitalist "democracies" are in no position to demand anything. Under the rule of monopoly capital it is not the consumer who demands the creation of the object of consumption—be it a hockey game or a president—but rather the object of consumption which demands the creation of the consumer—be he a "fan" or a "voter." Only in a socialist society, where production can be carried on first and foremost to fulfill (unmanipulated) human needs, and where the people can have actual control over the productive process itself, could the so-called consumer begin to be a *creator* of needs. In all of these spheres, from industry to sports to education to politics, this would entail breaking down the distinctions between controllers, producers, and consumers. In industry and politics—the apparent "distinction" between the two would disappear—we would have workers making decisions about their priorities at the point of production and electing mandated and immediately recallable delegates to the people's councils which would decide on overall social priorities. There would be no distinction between workers, consumers, and voters, nor any between workers and "political" leaders since the leaders would come from the ranks of the workers themselves. Similarly in the area of sports, one would insist on players' control over teams and the complete breakdown of the distinction between players and fans. Nearly everyone would become a player, and we would have a drastic reorientation from spectator to participation sports (and centering on the kinds of sports that *both* men and women could take part in together). Sports for the people.

Under capitalism the distorted and authoritarian social relations of production are the primary factors in dictating consumption. Also the visibility of this consumption—our day-in, day-out exposure to other people's consumption—becomes the second most powerful socializing force to further consumption. So sports consumption sells consumption generally. This is perhaps most obvious with the subsidiary and peripheral industries that have grown up around spectator sports. For example, sports like Olympic ice skating or skiing feed a huge skating and skiing industry. In her autobiography, Olympic ski champion Nancy Greene talks about how dependent Austria has become on the skiing industry, including, partly as a result of the habits of mind inculcated by spectator sports, such adjuncts as ski resorts, hotels and tourism. Then we have the whole host of other participation sports, from fishing to hunting to bowling to boating and so on, which together now comprise a multi-billion-dollar industry involving collectively almost all Americans. This society, which splits mental from manual labor, produces the phenomenon of "keeping in shape"—gymnasiums, weightlifting, beauty salons, diet foods, and the whole cult of the body. Then there are sports news and movies, sports clothes, sports cars, betting, shaving, men's deodorants and toiletry, the cult of the hard-drinking he-man to sell beer and liquor, and so forth.

One of the more obvious ways this works is shown in the burgeoning skiing industry. If you have looked through any ski magazines lately, you may find articles and ads resembling those in girlie mags. There has developed a whole cult of expensive ski resorts, fashionable ski ware, multicolored stretch pants, sun-tan oils, entertainment, cosmetics, sex—in short, the whole she-bang of what is called *"après* ski." In fact, what is being sold here is not a sport (or even a sports magazine), but a whole consumption-neurotic way of life. It re-minds one very much of what Herbert Marcuse, in *Eros and Civilization*, calls repressively desublimated sexuality—one is permitted a little skiing, or even a little sex, provided he pays for all the supposedly "neces-sary" hyperconsumption accessories.

Or take auto racing, a "sport" originally concocted to sell more cars. A recent article in the *Financial Post* (September 19, 1970) noted that Yardley of London (after shave) would be sponsoring the British Racing Motors Grand Prix team in an important meet. "We have become associated with auto racing," they quote a vice-president of Yardley, "because we consider it an extremely masculine sport, and quite frankly, we want this type of masculine association for our line of men's products." Other sponsors include Firestone Tires and Shell Oil (their stake in boosting the sex pro-file of automobiles should be obvious enough). The same *Financial Post* notes that the decision of Reynolds Metals Company, parent firm of Reynolds Aluminum, to sponsor the McLaren Can-Am racing team is equally simple: "About 70 per cent of the McLaren car's total weight is aluminum." (Ibid.) Similarly, in the same article an Imperial Tobacco official explained his com-pany's sponsorship of the Canadian Grand Prix: "Auto racing is a dynamic and exciting sport, and we feel this has been the right image for Player's cigarettes." He added that Player's sales go up during the Grand Prix period.

Another *Financial Post* article (March 14, 1970) took up the reasons why Air Canada decided to sponsor the recent world curling championships in Utica, New York. "We see curling becoming a major participating sport the world over," said a company executive. "And

this fits in with our role as a seller of transportation."
The writer adds that, "The airline believes amateur
athletes and their followers and families are significantly
responsible for increased air travel, not only to tournaments but to distant places for purely recreational
sports, such as a week of social golf."

As to hockey, "The endorsement of products by NHL
players has become big business in the past few years
and both [Commissioner] Campbell and [player repre-
sentative] Eagleson mention figures in the neighborhood of $500,000 annually as benefits to the players."
(Toronto *Telegram*, October 6, 1970.) The *Telegram's*
article went on to point out that the actual market in
the use of hockey stars to sell products was really many
times this size, since all sorts of companies have been
using hockey players' pictures or names without their
consent, and both the league and the players are de-
termined to put a stop to this so that they can cash in
on this aspect of the business. The league has set up its
own services division in New York to handle products
and endorsements, sticking the League's advertisements
on pennants, luggage, "official" skates, cups, sticks,
games, placards, shin guards, or what have you. They
even pursuaded General Mills, the makers of Wheaties,
to decorate fifteen million cereal boxes with hockey-
action pictures. "NHL glass was sold to General
Motors. Rexall Drugs signed a North America-wide endorsement as did the Gruen Watch Company. Other
sponsors include General Mills, Rawlings Sporting
Goods, Gerry Cosby and Co., Ovaltine Food Products,
Bauer Division of Greb Industries, etc., etc." (The
Toronto *Telegram*, November 16, 1970.)

In the ad-man era even individual sports stars have
had to have their images retooled. Take hockey's Dave
Keon. Another *Telegram* article (June 5, 1971) re-
gretted that, "Canadian athletes, and hockey players
in particular, have been behind Americans in establishment of a public image." So Keon had his image up-

lifted by the vice-president of a local radio station. "Let's face it," said the radio exec. "The time is right for Keon to cash in on his tremendous popularity . . . [to] be presented to the public as a speaker or a man to represent commercial products."

This brings us to that other main socializer for consumption—the mass media. As Marshall McLuhan has obliquely pointed out in his book *Understanding Media*, almost all news, views, and entertainment heard over the media are essentially advertisements for the consumption-oriented way of life favored by media advertisers and owners. Sports news, for one, has never really been much more than a bit of razzamatazz for promotional purposes, and the bribery of the mediamen by professional promoters has long been institutionalized. (In fact, listening to the sportscasters, it is impossible to differentiate them from sports promoters.) In his excellent book, *The Jocks*, Leonard Shecter remarks at one point that the so-called "Golden Age of Sport" in the '20s was a golden age of payola. He gives the example of Madison Square Garden impressario Tex Rickard who used to hand out $100 bills to deserving sportswriters. And he says, if things are less "golden" for sportswriters these days, it is only because the team owners realized they could be had for virtually nothing. "To hell with the newspapermen," ex-Mets boss George Weiss used to say. "You can buy them with a steak."

In the March 5, 1932 issue of *Collier's* magazine, heavyweight boxing champ Gene Tunney wrote that he paid 5 per cent of his fight purses to newsmen for publicity. He said it was the custom of most fighters to do likewise. And it is still commonplace for promoters to "hire" newsmen to be their press agents, often without even the knowledge of the newspaper editors: "These situations do not enhance the standing of the newspapers allowing such practice, nor do they establish in the minds of their readers . . . [anything

other than] the accusation of 'biased reporting.'"
(From an editorial entitled "Newsmen and 'Side' Jobs"
in *Editor and Publisher*.) Just before the 1964 Flint
Open Golf Tourney, all out-of-state reporters were offered the use of a Buick to drive to the match. Most
accepted. And, interestingly, the event was thereafter
announced in AP news dispatches as the "Buick Open."

Shecter points out that one reason reporters "easily
become what are called 'house men'" is that those
(very few) who occasionally tried to criticize a home
team have suddenly found themselves out of a job. He
cites various specific examples of this. Moreover, when
he himself uncovered the fact that in the '50s about
30 per cent of the basketball players at St. John's never
graduated, his paper, the New York *Post,* flatly refused
to print the story. Announcer Phil Rizzuto told the
Daily News that he does not "expect a guy to bite the
hand that feeds him" (i.e., an announcer to knock his
club), and so, too, may it be with newspapers and
clubs. Gelfand and Heath (op. cit.) who themselves
were former sportswriters, seem to have just discovered
this mutually profitable symbiosis. They insist, "Sports
editors should not forget that the more people they lead
into athletic activity, the more avid readers they re-
cruit." And Malcolm Mallette, associate director of the
American Press Institute adds, "Circulation managers
say that about 30% of the people who buy their papers
do it primarily for the sports news." (Parrish, op. cit.,
p. 109.) Such newspapers as the *Manchester Guardian,*
which are supposedly against gambling, have not been
loathe to carry point spreads and betting tips when they
thought it would boost their circulation. Shecter says
that the wedding of media sports departments and
sporting organizations has been so thoroughly consum-
mated that the two are often "partners." "There is the
real possibility," he adds, "that the newspaper needs
the team more than the team needs the newspaper."

In the case of pro football, this gives the owners—

a free multimillion-dollar propaganda machine with an influential voice in twenty-four major cities and population centers in the country. Almost on cue they promote a merger, push legislation, attack an opponent of the league, justify ticket-price increases, trades, and rule changes, or generally create a cover for whatever dealings the owners may be plotting . . . There is no question as to which side of their bread the butter is on . . . The glamorous aura that surrounds the owners and management was created by this crucial segment of the press and news media. It is as premeditated and calculating as the star system was in the motion-picture industry. (Parrish, op. cit., p. 108.)

National Football League Commissioner Pete Rozelle once remarked that "Whatever success the NFL has had is due, in no small measure, to the wholehearted support it has received through the years from newspapermen,[1] radio announcers and commentators, and, more recently, television announcers and commentators." Over the years one of the newspapers most friendly to the sports establishment has been the New York *Daily News*, America's largest-selling paper. The *Daily News* is also the long-time owner of television station WPIX, which has televised New York Yankee baseball for as long as I can remember (and now tele-

[1] "The commissioner has stocked the league office and other pork-barrel positions with former news wire-service men like Jim Kensil and Don Weiss from the Associated Press. Jack Hand from the AP is now head of NFL Films. Rozelle gets whatever he wants released through the wire services. The moral and, perhaps, legal question is how much is stopped or restricted to local areas to please him and the people he represents." (Parrish, op. cit., p. 111.) During the 1970 players' strike, the Players' Association found it practically impossible to answer the owners' well-publicized allegations because, according to Parrish, the wire services refused to print the players' press releases.

vises the New York Nets basketball games as well).
Thanks in part to sympathetic news coverage in the
Daily News, the Yanks and Nets can draw big TV audiences on WPIX, which can then raise its advertising
rates for the games. Which means more money in the
bank for the *Daily News.* This is not to say that the
Daily News doesn't treat the Mets and the Knicks every
bit as good as the Yanks and Mets. After all, the paper's
main sports "interest" is not its WPIX ad revenue, but
its daily circulation of around a million, including people it has trained to be good "fans" (and hence good
readers of the *News* sports pages).

The TV commentators are not far behind:

> In recent years, the trend has been toward the pro-
> fessional team selling radio and TV rights to a net-
> work, and in the process, having the privilege of
> selecting the announcers. The result has been the
> "All-America" announcer phenomenon [who, they
> say, is a "rooter," not a reporter] which, subtly or
> otherwise, promotes the home team and frequently
> reminds the listener to get his tickets for the next
> home game. (Gelfand and Heath, op. cit.)

"I'm a house man," sportscaster and ex-catcher Joe Garagiola reportedly used to say. "That's what they're
paying me to be." Phil Rizzuto, former All-Star short-
stop and now announcer for the New York Yankees,
was recently asked by the New York *Daily News* (August 22, 1971) how he feels when he hears reports that
announcers are just shills for the teams they work for.
"That's a lot of garbage," said the enthusiastic announcer. "I don't deny that I try to make the Yankees
sound interesting . . . [and] they do play many exciting
games and they do have some excellent ballplayers
. . . Sure I root for them, but what's wrong with that?
I don't go out of my way to knock the Yankees, but
what about these writers who knock the announcers?

Do you ever hear them knock the paper they write for?" (Or the paper's advertisers, we might add.)

But neither has the relationship between sportscasters and advertisers been anything other than loving. It wasn't so long ago that every time a home run sailed out of the park, the announcer would come on to tell you that the batter had hit a "Ballantine Blast," or a "White Owl Wallop," or a "Case of Wheaties," or a "Case of Lucky Strikes," or whatever the sponsor happened to be that day. (Finally, amidst a chorus of protest—none of which came from sportscasters—the baseball Commissioner had to remind his announcer jocks that, from now on "a home run will be called a home run.") Shecter points out that sports and TV "have become so inextricably entwined that sports *are* television and television *is* sports."

An article in the *Financial Post* of November 11, 1967, quoted John Bassett, publisher of the recently defunct Toronto *Telegram*, owner of the Toronto Argonauts and chairman of Maple Leaf Gardens, said, "You must educate your audience and merchandise your product, and this can be done through television." A similar story revealed that the Montreal Expos were producing a series of half-hour TV shows to "educate" their future fans, and they quote one club official: "We are particularly interested in attracting young people—high school and university students, for example—to ensure fans for the future." (*Financial Post*, March 1, 1969.)

Of course we should not delude ourselves that it is all a case of greedy promoters "using" the media. If anything, the symbiosis cuts mainly the other way. Shecter remarks, "Television *buys* sports. Television *supports* sports . . . So, slowly at first, but inevitably, television tells sports what to do. It *is* sports and runs them the way it does most other things, more flamboyantly than honestly."

In 1964 CBS outbid its rival networks for the rights

to televise National Football League games, and it seemed it would be beating NBC in the battle for Sunday afternoon viewers for years to come. So NBC "created" the American Football League. The AFL at that point was mainly a collection of inexperienced younger players and NFL discards, who seemed to be unable to play defense. Fumbles flew off in all directions. Their games often resembled comedy more than football. But NBC knew a shrewd investment when they saw one. They paid the AFL owners $38 million for a five-year TV contract, (compared with the just under $9 million ABC had paid for the AFL's previous five-year contract), and this was the money the new league used to battle the old for the pick of the most promising rookies. "We couldn't have competed," said AFL Commissioner Joe Foss, "without television." And sure enough, with NBC putting up a good part of the bankroll, the new league became almost as strong as the old, and NBC had a valuable product on its hands.

"If you don't watch those TV people," says former Boston Celtics basketball coach Bill Russell, "they will devour you. First they ask you to call time-outs so they can get in their commercials. Then they tell you *when* to call them. Then they want to get into the locker room at half time. Then more and more. If you don't put on the brakes, they'll tell you when to play." (Of course Russell made these statements five years ago. Now television *does* tell sports teams when to play— for example, we have ABC's $7.5 million schedule of Monday night pro football.)

There has been a lot of hullabaloo about TV breaking up games to get in commercials. The TV people have always denied it. However, in May 1967, pro soccer referee Peter Rhodes admitted that he was required to wear an electronic beeper on his shoulder, and when the network (CBS) signaled, he had to signal an "injury," thus allowing time for a commercial. In her autobiography, Nancy Greene talks about how the schedule of the Olympic Games tended to be divided to suit the convenience of the TV boys.

But television controls not just when games are played, but *whether* they are played at all and *how* they are played. Simply by giving coverage to some sports rather than others, TV can help ensure that those will be the popular ones. Pro football, to take one example, struggled along as a sort of freak show of overgrown collegians until TV "created" it as a sport in the militarized era of the Cold War. In some recent football All-Star games, TV is said to have "prohibited" red dogging the quarterback, in order to give the viewing audience a more wide open spectacle. Shecter says the main reason the Milwaukee Braves were willing to go through the tremendous hassles of moving to Atlanta was that it was a much more lucrative TV market. Similarly, improved TV subsidies were said to be the reason the National Hockey League expanded from six to twelve teams. It was television that uncovered pro soccer from the American sandlots and gave it national coverage. Without TV, "sports" like the roller derby and professional wrestling could not have survived. And it was ABC television—that most patriotic of networks—that concocted its own heavyweight championship elimination tournament to fill the "vacant" throne of Muhammed Ali.[2]

[2] Lately ABC has come up with its own new-and-improved brand of hip sports promoter in Howard Cosell, a man whose supposed "tell it like it is" commentary on sports telecasts does not prevent him from ballyhooing and promoting the ritual with every second word. It reminds you very much of the "damning" critiques of jockery by men like Jim Bouton and John Sample who, if you read their books, turn out to accept 99.9 per cent of the jock mythology. Not surprisingly, after his hotly debated, but cream-puff, critiques of major league baseball, Bouton, too, had little trouble landing himself a network TV sports job, with ABC in New York no less.

In 1970, Bernie Parrish notes, "Chrysler alone spent more than $13 million to sell their cars to pro football's selective audience of 18–49 age-group males in the wholesome setting provided by pro football." But, since the spectacular costs of sponsoring the games *are* worth it in terms of reaching the most lucrative buying markets, these huge sponsorship costs become one more barrier a smaller company would have to surmount in order to stay in business. In this way, the huge scale of the burgeoning sports-TV business acts as a tremendous stimulant to the growth of monopoly in American business generally.

The amounts of money changing hands in all this are simply staggering. CBS is paying out about $25 million a year for rights to televise pro football. And they more than get it back from the advertisers. At last count, advertising costs for sponsors of the Super Bowl were approaching two hundred thousand dollars for *a minute* of commercial time! Of course, only the biggest corporations in America can afford the costs. The automobile corporations are high on the list (using "manhood" to sell cars).

John Galbraith, in his book *The New Industrial State* has perceptively noted, "The industrial system is profoundly dependent on commercial television and could not exist in its present form without it." This is certainly true for the modern mammoth sports industry. But the reverse is to some extent true as well: It is doubtful if commercial television could have grown as fast, or could exist in its present form, without the sports industry. In his treatise on "The Long Range Effects of TV and Other Factors on Sports Attendance," Jerry N. Jordan cites research proving that, "sports-minded people, because of their great interest in competitive games, were among the first to buy television sets." TV companies were advertising such things as, "Your TV set is your ticket on the 50-yard line," or "Enjoy the game in comfort in your home regardless of the weather," and so on. He notes that in 1948, the first year that television sets were being mass produced, the percentage of TV time devoted to sports was sometimes as high as 35 per cent, and over the year averaged 16 per cent. Even now the most common plug for color TV buying is the suggestion that you can see the game in color. Similarly, both pro sports owners and pay-TV companies are hoping sports can usher in the new super-gravy era of pay TV and profits for them both. So the general rule is that television needs sports almost as much as sports needs television. In the era of monopoly capitalism both have the function of stimulating hyperconsumption and fronting for the mass advertiser, from whom both industries ultimately get most of their financial backing and, therefore, by whom they are ultimately controlled. (It should be pointed out that these advertising costs are added on to the price of consumer goods, so that ultimately the working class is forced to pay the price of its own brainwashing.) Monopoly capitalism needs monopoly capitalist sports and vice versa. The material conditions that create the one also create the other.

As we have shown, sports watching helps to develop the sort of passive, acquisitive stance that favors escape or pseudo satisfaction through consumption generally. If a guy is dumb enough to identify with a ball team, why not with a brand-name beer. ("Baseball and Ballantine. Baseball and Ballantine . . ." is the little jingle that started all New York Yankee baseball telecasts for many years.) And if a guy is desperate enough to look for his manhood in a ball park, why not in a department store? Sports machismo is good business. If you can keep the guys hustling after the brass ring of "manliness," you can sell them everything from "a man's deodorant" to "sports cars with drive."

In the last analysis all this is based, not on any special idiocy of the sports world, not even on any special deviousness of mass advertisers, but on the social rela-

tions of capitalist production itself. A guy who has to
look for his humanity identifying with the supermasculine menials of his team obviously is not one who's
engaged in creative decision making and control of work
he can really believe in. Turned into a cog on a job he
does not believe in, with a woman whom the system has
turned into another cog—or even worse a housewife—
his sex life is not likely to be all that great either. So
he chases his manhood—or the illusion of it—where he
may, more or less like a hungry mouse in a maze. In
the final analysis, the success of sports promoters, or
promoters generally, is based, not on their ability to
inculcate "false" needs in people (as Marcuse, for one,
seems to believe), but on their ability to turn *genuine*
needs, which the capitalist system cannot satisfy, into
vehicles for selling their products.[3] Until there is workers' control over industrial production, and until that
production is reoriented toward serving unmanipulated
human needs rather than the accumulation of profits,
people will continue to seek their humanity in commodities.

[3] A good example of this is the commercial often heard
during pro football games for Tijuana Smalls cigars—a jingle
repeats again and again "With Tijuana Smalls, you know
who you are, you know who you are." The point is that the
average American fan does *not* know who he is. This system
has turned him into a cipher, and in the back of his mind he
knows it.

> . . . there were gymnastics—especially women's gymnastics, the girlie show of sport.
>
> *Sports Illustrated* coverage of the Mexico Olympics
>
> Miss Hattiesburg High '67, National Sweetheart of Theta Kappa Omega, Mississippi Junior Miss, Ole Miss Top Beauty, Miss America Hopeful
>
> titles of a recent University of Mississippi cheerleader

8

School for Sexism

Sexual apartheid in sports originates from more or less the same roots as the racial apartheid in the sports of South Africa. Both were established on the sports fields of England's all-white, all-boys public schools which originated our kinds of team sports in the nineteenth century. No, despite what you might read in the British press, sports apartheid in South Africa was not an Afrikaner invention. It derives from the English-speaking private schools, universities, and such clubs as the Wanderers in Johannesburg, many of which have played their part to this day in keeping that country's international teams lily white. The most obvious reason blacks and women were excluded from English public school sports is that they were not admitted to

these schools in the first place. The function of these
places was properly to train and socialize an all-white,
all-male imperial ruling class. Team sports were one
way the elite was more solidly welded together. And
since it was a male elite that was going to be tough-
ened up for their role as world imperialists, perhaps the
most popular of the early team sports turned out to be
the ultra-macho game of rugby. Now in rugby, perhaps
even more than its American successor football, the
broken bones come so fast and furious that this "game"
might better be called a kind of carnage. Even after
it spread beyond the public schools, or got watered
down into American football, it was obviously not a
game for women. The public school team sports were
part of the socialization process whereby the male
Angle-Saxon elite learned to recognize one another,
and use their elite exclusionist sports as a preparation
for their more general notions of elitist rule.[1]

Sports like cricket and rugby were, thus, part of the
ideological-social cement that welded the male ruling
class together. Other exclusively male bonds were the
exclusionist men's clubs, men's activities like gam-

[1] Largely, the same has been true for America's prep
schools and exclusive men's clubs. For example, among New
York City's most elite clubs are The Links (a former golf
club), the Racquet and Tennis Club, and the New York
Yacht Club. In many cities the Jockey Club is a place where
no jockey has ever set foot.

It's also worth noting that almost all of the elite sports
are oriented to the *individual,* rather than team, performance,
and that players on both sides were "whites." Even in the
team games, the home team customarily wears *white* uniforms. And in the recent Fischer-Spassky World Chess Championship, *Time* magazine (July 31, 1972) depicted its national favorite son Fischer as a *white* chess piece and the
Russian Spassky as a brown (Negro?) one; several TV networks did likewise. A neat combination of national chauvinism, elitism, and racism.

bling, men's prerogatives to "serious" conversation (and monopolization of "unladylike" subjects like politics), and the widespread belief that sex was simply a woman's "marital duty" (which only her husband was supposed to enjoy). The new all-male sporting traditions formed part of this ideological base behind which men—and especially the male ruling class which originated these activities—got themselves solidified and gradually extended their exclusionist monopoly over more and more areas of meaningful life. The frivolous and household pursuits could then be safely left to the "ladies."

Even today sports remain one of the prime ways young men are brought together (even though they might be competing against one another), while comparable girls' pursuits, like playing with dolls, learning to be housekeepers, shopping, or whatever, are for the most part carried out in the comparative social isolation of separate households. The boys gather the contacts that will enable them to dominate society, while the girls slowly acquire the habit of living through their menfolk. Over and above these rationales for the exclusion of women was the general male supremacist and anti-sexual atmosphere of the Victorian era in which the team sports developed. (Particularly ironic because a woman male supremacist sat on the throne.) There, of course, remained the strong suspicion in those times that any unnecessary contact between the sexes was bound to lead to damnation. To have them playing sports together might well bring down the Empire.

And to this day the world of jockery still maintains a vividly anti-female aura. In their book *Modern Sportswriting*, Gelfand and Heath casually remind their readers that, "Some news pictures of female tennis players are chosen by deskmen primarily because they have more sex appeal than other pictures available."

An article by Melvin Durslag in the Toronto *Star* was headed

Sex Appeal
Invaded Tennis

and discussed, among other things, the efforts of professional tennis promoter Bobby Riggs to "cash in" on Gussie Moran's panties. "When Jack [Kramer] played on the Riggs tour, he earned no more than Gussie Moran . . . on the logical ground that Gussie's legs were worth as much as Jack's serve." Similarly, Harlem Globetrotters impressario Abe Saperstein came up with a stimulating extra for his show: "During the intermission, Saperstein would match the Golden Goddess of Tennis, Karol Fageros, who had a shape that should only happen to your girl, against Althea Gibson. 'What the Trotters need,' said Abe, 'is sex appeal.'" In short, such female participation in sport as there is is treated as just another girlie show.

In the sexually repressed atmosphere that makes such attitudes possible, the male athletes don't fare that well either.

In his book *Ball Four* (pp. 36–38), Jim Bouton gives the almost unbelievably sick details of one of major league baseball's most popular pastimes—"beaver shooting." This involves such things as sneaking under the seating of stadiums, "so that to the tune 'The Star-Spangled Banner' an entire baseball club of clean-cut American boys would be looking up the skirt of some female." Other common Peeping Tom techniques used by ballplayers include "peering over the top of the dug-out to look up dresses," hanging from fire escapes to look into windows, drilling holes in walls, or holding a mirror under the crack of a hotel-room door. Bouton admits that some people might look down on this sort of thing. "But in baseball if you shoot a particularly good beaver, you are a highly respected person, one might even say a folk hero of sorts." He tells about one hotel

that had various L-shaped wings which made it particularly vulnerable to beaver shooting from the roof.
"The Yankees would go up there in squads of fifteen or
so, often led by Mickey Mantle himself." If anybody
spotted something, "there'd be a mad scramble of guys
climbing over the skylights, tripping over each other
and trying not to fall off the roof." Just after Bouton
joined the Yankees, and found himself up on the roof
with the team at 2:30 in the morning, he recalls saying
to himself, "So this is the big leagues." It resembles
much more the sexual deprivation of early adolescence.
Imagine; our great American sports heroes have so little opportunity to make love to American woman-
hood that they have to play peekaboo on rooftops and
fire escapes just to catch a glimpse of a female body.

   In fact, the sort of drooling, Peeping Tom atmosphere
seems to have penetrated almost every aspect of competitive sports. In 1971 the cameramen at the ABC-
NCAA telecasts of college football would every once
and a while beaver shoot a particularly fetching lady
at the game, and captions like "Not that bad," or
"Strong!" would flash across the TV screen underneath
her picture. The Enden Shampoo commercials for the
professional games were more of the same. The general idea was that football heroes who use Enden will
always reel in the beautiful girls. Like big Ben Davidson who reels in three of them in one commercial. Or
Alex Karras who warns you solemnly against the perils
of being a loser, and then points to his beautiful girl,
saying, "She's no loser! She's got me!"

   But even when the players manage to get into bed
with one of their "baseball Annies" or other "easy lays,"
they are not much better off:

   The artificial light falling on false eyelashes, oily cosmetics and the smell of cigarette smoke inclined me
   toward sexual depression. The attention we got from
   those women (and men too) was sad. The frustra-

tion of a stagnant society drained them. There was
nothing left but to suck energy from each other and
from us. No matter how they tried to disguise it, it
always looked shabby and sordid to me. (Chip
Oliver, op. cit., p. 117.)

The sexual repression (including the sexual repression of compulsive cosmetics sexuality) is beaten right
into the players along with the sports. They are supposed to be clean livers: not too many women; bed-
check at 11:00 P.M.; and, of course, no sex within at
least forty-eight hours of the game. The superstition
is that sex weakens you. Physiologically, this is sheer
nonsense. If anything, a little healthy love making gets
rid of tensions, clears the mind, and may even rein-
vigorate the body. But what it does "weaken" is those
sado-masochistic tensions which come from sexual repression, which might make one hard-hitting killer on
a football field. And, more generally, if athletes were
less sexually deprived, they would certainly be far less
willing to take orders from despotic coaches and managers. The atmosphere of a pro training camp, suggests
a kind of "jock convent." Whether they know it or not,
"male" sports are one of the things that have made the
jocks accomplices in their own sexual (and, hence, political) repression.

"Judging from the behavior of many high-school athletic coaches, and even the way the plant is designed,"
writes Edgar Friedenburg, in his introduction to
Howard Slusher's *Man, Sport and Existence* (Philadelphia: Lea and Febiger, 1967), "the characteristic attitude of physical education instruction toward the body,
and the joy it may yield, is not merely repressive—it is
truly counterphobic. It is the 'phys ed' men, typically,
who are the school disciplinarians—who snarl at 'wise
guys' and put down 'troublemakers.' It is they among
teachers who show the most hostility to boys with long
hair or odd, mod dress, and who encourage the mem-

bers of their teams to harass these youths." And he says that if the "gung-ho" jocks can be provoked into assaulting the long hairs, the school authorities use the incident as an excuse for coming down hard on all forms of "permissiveness" in life style or dress. Moreover, high school authorities themselves tend to be recruited increasingly from former phys ed personnel. Friedenburg says they bring to their lofty positions "the spirit of the informal martinet, superficially jolly but intolerant of spirit in young people and of poetry in anything—especially in athletics itself."

American society's general prohibitions against men touching men, or women touching women—or either sex touching the other in any way that doesn't lead straight into bed ("a pass")—works to channel sexuality into the narrow bounds of genital-to-genital intercourse. Men are further prohibited from showing any real emotion, so that even intercourse becomes for many a part of the act of "staying cool." More than that, it becomes the main arena of the constant battle to "prove" what is defined (especially by such writers as Norman Mailer) as one's "masculinity." The battle is fought on the playing fields, too, especially in the ultra-macho game of football. Here, as we've said, it's a particularly narrow kind of "masculinity," the kind measured in brawn not brain, in scoring those touchdowns. The next time you watch a pro football game try to count the number of times the announcer calls out the weights of the players, particularly the big burly interior linemen. "And there's big Ben Davidson tipping the scales at two hundred and eighty pounds . . . And there's Bob Lilly, a solid two-sixty pounds of beef . . ." You might think they were calling out the weights of prize calfs at a cattle show. Men reduced to slabs of beef. Depicted as heavyweight *objects*. It's the male equivalent of the way they describe bathing "beauties" and cheerleaders.

An unusually perceptive article in the Toronto *Tele-*

gram's Weekend Magazine noted, "football represents the deep-seated desire of every red-blooded American male to be a Superman, all-powerful and immortal . . . the average man's ultimate trip, the fulfillment of the American dream." On the other hand:

> Cheerleaders and baton twirlers, for their part, typify pure American womanhood. There's a hint of good, clean sex in their short skirts and well-rounded sweaters, mind you—but the image is strictly virginal. The message is: Look, don't touch.
>
> In fact, the male's attempt to prove his superiority is very much in evidence. Cheerleaders are relegated to a position of worshipping at the altar of a ritual they can never really be part of.

Football is America's No. 1 fake-masculinity ritual, and the worshipping females are used to give the mock ritual its validity. More than that, the cheerleaders' tiny skirts and rounded sweaters also help inject the proper tension into the atmosphere. They are the modern day equivalent of the Vestal Virgins that the Romans maintained to bless their mass gladiatorial spectacles.

As a symbol of just how much sexuality has been subordinated to the demands of the production ethic, the only time one player is allowed to touch another in a friendly way is when he has just scored a touchdown. Nor does the brutalization of sexuality end with the game. It is even visible in the attitude of the athletes toward their wives. "I'm really gonna *punish* my ole lady tonite," declared one pro footballer. "Put the wood to her. Make 'er suffer." It is as if the jocks were so brutalized on their jobs that one of the few consolations left to them was having the upper hand with their wives. They certainly do not have it with their coaches. So sexism becomes an opiate for political repression.

It is no secret that around such sexually repressed all-male terrains as locker rooms, boys prep schools, or prisons, women are just "cunts," "gash," "pieces of ass."

(It's as if sex had to be dirty to be any fun.) Even the verbiage of a football game goes hand in hand with that of a brutalized sexuality: "Ramming into the middle . . . sliding into the pocket . . . smashing in . . . beating . . . thrashing . . ." The words for brutalized sex seem to be the same as those for brutalized sports, and are used by the athletes for both. Similarly, the movements of the cheerleaders are plugged into what amounts to a set of stereotyped military drill routines. Watching the drum majorettes and girls' drill teams prancing about in their mini-skirted mock uniforms, in precision goose steps, it is hard to miss the symbolism of sexuality subordinated to militarism, sexuality used as an advertisement for militarism, and frustrated sexuality used as a spur to militarism and machismo generally.

It is obvious that college and professional footballers would not go through endless hours of agonizing calisthenics and brutalizing scrimmages under the yoke of fascist coaches for money alone. Nor do pro hockey players crack each other's bones with their sticks for "love of the game." Nor do boys run themselves ragged to play on varsity teams because they like "clean living." None of this could happen without the spur of intra-male competition—the endless dog-eat-dog struggle to be the biggest jock (cock?) on the block. Sports is one of the central arenas in which this struggle—with all its physical and, especially, *mental* brutality—is carried out. (Never mind that the wealth and power that make a player subservient to an owner are not even at stake.) This is the competiton behind the competition. "This," we are told, "is where they separate the Men from the boys."

In his article on "Masculine Inadequacy and Compensatory Development of Physique," Robert G. Harlow noted that various observations on the characteristic behavior of weight lifters suggested an "abnormal accentuation" of certain signs of masculinity. In particular, the secondary masculine characteristics—such as brawn—became for these men the very criteria of their manhood, and:

> . . . in general, the weight lifter is characterized by excessive anxiety concerning his masculine adequacy; that his weight lifting and subsequent strength and physique development are attempts to demonstrate both to himself and to others his male potency. (*Contemporary Readings in Sport Psychology*, William P. Morgan, ed., 1970.)

He notes that, whereas thirty years ago the number of American men interested in weight training could be counted in hundreds, there are at least a million men interested in it now. This just might provide some index of the rise of feelings of masculine inadequacy and macho generally in today's militarized society (though it should be noted that other important reasons for this are the further fragmentation and bureaucratization of work, and the tremendous growth in the past thirty years of advertising and mass media that use feelings of sexual inadequacy as a vehicle to sell products).

Of course the intra-male competition is bigger than all the sports fields. It goes on in all its brutality in bars, swingles clubs, factories, offices, prisons—anywhere and everywhere that men who have been denied control over their jobs and lives gather. Instead of struggling against those forces that keep us all—black and white, men and women, young and old, long hair and short— in subservience to the power of capital, the frustrations and aggressions get turned inward into a misdirected competition of each oppressed male against every other in a never-ending rat race for the prize of "masculinity." In his aptly titled book *The Prisoner of Sex*, Mailer admits that this race never ends. No matter how many times the prisoners debase themselves and their women to "prove their masculinity," it isn't enough. Each day the contest begins anew—it's very much like sports—and the prisoners have to prove themselves yet again. One wonders why the Mailers of this world continue to run.

No doubt they think it's a basic law of nature that things should be this way. It is true that anthropologists have discovered varying degrees of intra-male competition in most—though not all—human societies. But this competition, where it exists, is clearly defined and modulated by the institutions of the particular society in which it occurs. (Just like sports, eating, wearing clothes, or anything else.) Under the rule of monopoly capital the monopolization of the means of production by the few at the top leads to a hypercompetition for goods and status by those at the bottom. This, in turn, is tremendously magnified by the bureaucratization and fragmentation of work under this system, and by the fact that overproduction for profit (apart from any demonstrable human need) encourages the monopolists to further stimulate the competition, vis-à-vis sexist advertising. Sex, like everything else in such a society, is turned into a commodity. And the competition for sex is rigged from the very beginning. Sex is allotted the impossible task of somehow making up for meaningless, alienated work. And the competition for sex, like all other competitions, is arranged so that there can only be a few winners, and under this system even they can never win (consume) enough. So they have to run anew every day.

Women are the prizes of this game. Without sexual repression, no game. No intra-male competition, a stronger and more united proletariat. Hence, no capitalism. To keep the system going, you have to—in so far as possible—keep the women out of the game. Play up the "differences" between men and women. Keep the women off to the side. Outside production. Off the field. And, besides, if you had men and women tackling each other on the playing field of this sexually repressed society, they might like it so much that they'd just ad-

journ to the bedrooms. You couldn't get anyone to play
the game. You couldn't get anyone to work. You
couldn't get anyone to take orders. End of game.

The argument is often made that, because of bio-
logical differences (admittedly exaggerated by socialization) women are simply not able to stand the faster,
more bruising, pace of many of today's male sports.
This may well be true. But what if we should decide
that this fast, bruising hypercompetitive pace of many
male sports is simply too sick, brutalizing, and oppressive to the jocks themselves? Couldn't we have less brutal sports that both men and women could play
together? (Mixed doubles in tennis might be one example.) And, if the women didn't play 100 per cent as
"well" as the men, why should anybody even care! In
fact, why bother with scoring or winning the game at
all? Wouldn't it be enough just to enjoy it?

Times are changing. In February 1970 a major
ruckus erupted when a thirty-one-year-old mother of
two applied for the job of assistant football coach at
Idaho State University. (The school's athletic director
allowed as that, while he "sympathized with the
women's liberation movement," he decided "to stick
with tradition and hire a man.") The case drew national
publicity. In August Patricia Palinkas became the first
woman to play professional football. She did the holding for her husband Steve, placekicker for the Orlando
Panthers in the Atlantic Coast League. A burly linebacker for the Bridgeport team promptly tried to end
her career on her very first play. "I tried to break
her neck," declared the 235-pound linebacker. (Pat
Palinkas weighs 122 pounds.) "I don't know what she's
trying to prove. I'm out here trying to make a living
and she's out here prancing around making folly with
a man's game." One could hardly expect a thick-headed
linebacker to realize that his brutalization was directly
related to the absence of women from his "man's

game." In any case, Ms. Palinkas shook off the pounding and continued to play.

In September women tennis players threatened to boycott Jack Kramer's Pepsi Pacific Southwest tournament. They claimed that, of $65,000 in prize money, only $7,500 was earmarked for the women's events. Ironically, it wasn't long before black tennis star Arthur Ashe—often depicted as a fierce campaigner for equality—was drawn into the fray. On the side of the promoters! There could be few more graphic examples of the system's ability to divide working people who should be united. Male and female tennis players, both of whom, after all, are being given the short end of the purse by the promoters, end up fighting, not with the bosses, but with each other. Arthur Ashe, who has himself been the victim of racist discrimination, expressed the view that women players should not be getting anything more than what they already do. "Men are doing this for a living now," said Ashe. "They have families, and they don't want to give up money just for girls to play." (This is precisely the sort of short-sighted attitude expressed by some white working men who fear that they might lose their jobs if their trades are opened up to blacks. They don't realize that their low pay and poor working conditions are based in part on the bosses' ability to use one section of the working class as a reserve army of labor or cheap work force against the other—or, in the case of non-working housewives, as a barrier against their husband's ability to go on strike.) Ashe also claimed that, "Only three or four women draw fans to a tourney, anyhow, so why do we have to split our money with them?" This is analogous to racist bosses who claim that, "Hardly any Negroes are qualified, so why should they get better jobs?" Both statements are badly misleading. If it is true that blacks are sometimes less qualified (qualified for what?), most people would concede that racist inferior education was at fault. Similarly, if women tennis players are poorer draws than men, might not a good part of the reason be the macho-oriented treatment they get from the media, which consistently subordinate women's tennis to men's? (Also, the usual practice of tennis promoters to reserve the center courts for men's matches tends to perpetuate a situation in which the men's matches are assumed to be more important and, hence, a better draw. Similarly, as long as whites monopolize the better jobs they will tend to be the "best qualified" for them.) The women tennis pros refused to accept the racist rationales dished up to them in the news media, and decided instead to organize their own series of tournaments separate from those of the official promoters. (Ironically, though, at least five of the feminist tournies were to be sponsored by the makers of Virginia Slims who sought to cash in on women's liberationist sentiment by marketing a cigarette created especially for women with the slogan, "You've come a long way, baby." And soon the women's tournies were every bit as commercialized as the men's.)

At about the same time women's golf pro Carol Mann made news by engaging in a special match at Grossinger's with Doug Sanders. Women jockeys broke into horse racing. Women runners competed in the Boston marathon. (The Amateur Athletic Union, which "owns" the race, refused them "official status," claiming long-distance running would be injurious to a woman's health.)

As of this writing, a minor league umpire named Bernice Gera was suing the bigwigs of baseball, charging that she has been denied umpiring jobs for which she is qualified because of sex discrimination. (The alleged reason for excluding her was that, as a big league ump, she would have to hear all sorts of coarse "unladylike" language.) The case was debated in characteristically hilarious fashion by sportscaster Joe Garagiola on the "Joey Bishop Show." Typically, Garagiola took his stand with the baseball establishment. At first, the sportscaster and ex-catcher tried to bluff his way through the issues with his usual repetoire of "jokes." He couldn't really conceive that a woman could be qualified for the job. Pressed by Bishop, he added that even if she meets all the requirements, he still didn't think she belongs. (Garagiola had also testified on the owner's behalf in Curt Flood's test case of the reserve clause, calling the reserve system necessary.) Joey Bishop, who has apparently never learned the ways of jockery, took the view that "prejudice" and "discrimination" were probably involved in the Gera case. The audience applauded. Perhaps some people are becoming aware that the fight against machismo and sexism is a necessity for *both* men and women. Even for jocks.

Of course, it is important to see that the fight against sexism in sports, or in society generally, is *not* won by fitting a few females into the slots of the same repressive system (in this case, the same macho sports). It is hard to see what great benefits black people derived from being "allowed" to make it into professional sports. In fact, at a recent symposium at Queens College in New York, one of the leaders of the black movement in sports, Harry Edwards, said that in his opinion blacks had been deceived into an overemphasis on sports. The irony is, then, that black liberationists seem to be withdrawing from sports at the same moment as women's liberationists are clamoring to get in. The apparent incongruity will be resolved only if the mass participation of women in sports is geared to changing the distorted, ultra-macho character of the sports themselves. What we don't need is a new generation of *female* gladiators.

We have seen how the system of monopoly capitalism is responsible for hypercompetition among the oppressed, for militarism, for the brutalization of play and of sex; how it reifies labor power and turns workers (including ballplayers) into commodities; how it turns

men and women into sexual objects, and then uses
their uptightness about their sexual marketability to
sell them products ranging from deodorants to ball
games. We have seen how play—something which we
might define as spontaneous sensuous practice performed for its own sake and the immediate enjoyment
of the players—was turned into the *business* of organized sports; how this subordinated to the work ethic
what we might metaphorically call the "play impulse."
In organized capitalist sports, play becomes alienated
work, because someone is making a profit from it.

Similarly with sex. Here the hegemony of alienated
work over play results in the brutalization of love. The
wholesale mutilation of human abilities effected by this
system is perhaps most apparent in its sociopsychological dimensions. The hegemony of alienated work over
play is mirrored, on the psychological level, in the
hegemony of the Reality Principle (or work ethic) over
the Pleasure Principle, of ego over id, of "masculinity"
over "femininity," of authority over desire, of sado-
masochism over sexuality. In modern automated industrial society, for the first time in human history, the
material wherewithal is available to abolish all forms
of scarcity and toil, to turn alienated labor for profit
and external ends into creative work, enjoyable in and
of itself, and thus to break down the barrier between
work and play. Nevertheless, because the ruling elite
of monopoly capitalist society has a vested interest in
continued alienated labor for their continued power
and profit, not only is alienated work not abolished,
but its fruits are more and more intensively used to
dominate the working peoples of the world and ensure
the system's continuation. At the present time the
United States is spending $80 billion a year on its mili-
tary apparatus alone. And even more money is poured
down the drain of waste consumption on things like
cars and cosmetics, which the people have been
taught to need so that the system of alienated labor

for private profit might continue. And even the whole advertising-mass media brainwashing complex is paid for by the people out of higher prices of their consumer goods. It was pointed out by Herbert Marcuse in *Eros and Civilization* in 1955 that as the material where-withal to do away with scarcity and alienated labor gradually came into being, the maintenance of this out-dated form of social order would require greater and greater degrees of repression—not just police and legal repression, but psychological repression as well.

Now in Freudian psychology the term "repression" has a rather specific meaning. It describes the process that takes place in childhood whereby sexual energy is "sublimated" (i.e., reallocated) in order to be available to meet the demands of work, and, more generally, of non-genital, social, and intellectual life. However, Marcuse pointed out that in a society of alienated labor a *surplus amount of repression* (over and above that required for civilization) has to be exacted in order to keep the populace doing the same alienated tasks in the service of private capital. Furthermore, as the so-ciety moved closer and closer toward having the means to do away with alienated labor entirely, the degree of surplus repression required would greatly increase, and unless something were done to short-circuit this process, this increased (and increasingly unnecessary) predatory domination of the ego-superego over the id (over the possibility of work becoming play) would dramatically increase "personal" (i.e., socially caused) frustration and aggression, brutalization and destruc-tiveness. This is what is now happening, both on the sports fields and in the bedrooms. It shows itself in the increasing brutalization of both play and love.

According to Freudian psychology, the means by which sexual repression is effected by the present so-ciety is through the operation of the incest taboo within the present nuclear family structure. The male child's "Oedipal" love for his mother is forcibly repressed by his father and diverted into mere affection, in particular the special affection due to Motherhood. The sexual repression that takes place in this process places the Pleasure Principle under the hegemony of the Reality Principle, the pleasure-oriented id under the hegemony of the repressed ego, and makes repressively sublimated sexual energy available for work. Sexuality and play must thereafter come second to alienated work. Moreover this Oedipal repression introduces a split into the male child's consciousness between those for whom it is permissible to have explicitly sexual feelings, and those toward whom—like Mother—it is not. This leads directly into the dichotomy between back-street and pedestal women for whom one either may or may not have sexual feelings. And from this it follows that a good deal of male sexual practice consists of degrading women ("cunts") to the point where it is permissible to have sexual feelings for them. In the vast majority of cases, actual male sexual performance becomes an act of sadistic masturbation in which the man imagines he is sadistically dominating his partner (or, often, even having a sadistic orgy which his back-street woman). Male impotence in marriage is almost always caused by the inability to degrade the wife to the stature of a back-street woman because one has identified her with Mother.

And similarly with female children. There the "Electral" love the little girl feels for her father is similarly, but less intensely, repressed by him. Here the amount of repression is less (and the little girl is unable to identify with her repressor); so the girl is less authoritarian, productivity-oriented, and directed toward dominance and sado-masochism than her brother. But her sexuality is only slightly less effectively split than his, and thereafter sexual performance for her is apt to be masochistic masturbation. In both cases, though, it is important to note, the "justification" for the repression is the maintenance of the nuclear family (a kind of family nationalism, and precursor of all other forms of nationalism) and the diversion of sexual energy into the service of the work ethic, including the surplus repression necessary for alienated work, the sadistic-macho orientation of the he-man, dominance-tripping football player and the almost masochistic passivity of his worshipping cheerleaders.

The relation between the incest taboo, split sexuality, and sado-masochism was not something discovered by modern-day feminists. It was, in fact, something of which Freud himself was painfully aware:

> . . . we shall not be able to deny that the behavior in love of the men of present-day civilization bears in general the character of the psychically impotent type. In only very few people of culture are the two strains of tenderness and sensuality duly fused into one: the man almost always feels his sexual-activity hampered by his respect for the woman and only develops full sexual potency when he finds himself in the presence of a lower type of sexual object . . . (Freud, "The Most Prevalent Form of Degradation in Erotic Life," in his *Collected Papers*, London: Hogarth Press, 1950, Vol. IV, p. 210.)

Freud felt compelled, reluctantly, to accept the pain and suffering caused by this split, psychopathic sexuality and the accompanying sadistic aggression, impotence, and neurosis. For Freud the ultimate rationale for sexual repression and all its agony was "economic; since [society] has not means enough to support life for its members without work on their part, it must see to it that the number of these members is restricted and their energies directed away from sexual activities on to their work." (*A General Introduction to Psychoanalysis*, New York: Garden City Publishing Co., 1943, p. 273.)

But what if the means of production of society had developed to the point that made repressive work unnecessary? What if work might be done creatively for its own sake, like play? As this point approached men and women would be less and less willing to do alienated drudge work, less and less willing to have their play turned into work, less and less prepared to be repressed in traditional sexist sex roles, and less and less satisfied by the traditional agonies of split sexuality and degradation. As the surplus repression exacted to fulfill an authoritarian work ethic becomes less and less justifiable, the old repressions and the traditionally accepted sexual horrors they lead to become more and more painful. At this point there are two possible paths. One can work to replace the old authorities, establish the society organized on the principle of to each according to his needs (i.e., post-scarcity communism), and liberate the new possibilities for sensuous fulfillment (including work that becomes play). Or one can cling to the old authorities, the old society, and the old repressive Reality Principle (in which one has such a painful investment of sexual repression and frustration) and become virulently anti-communist. The first path tends toward socialism. The second toward fascism. The fascist path requires increased amounts of waste consumption to mask the fact that scarcity and repression are no longer necessary. It requires increased political repression (i.e., law and order) to keep the more sexually and politically aware young in their place, and provide sadistic destructive outlets for the frustrations created by this increasingly irrational surplus sexual repression. It requires a foreign enemy, and a domestic scapegoat. The latter requirement leads to an upsurge of racism.

When you are the anvil you bend. But when you are the hammer you strike.

A black "rioter" at Attica state prison in New York.

It's insulting to me that I don't see more black coaches . . . any black managers in baseball, any black head coaches in football playing the game. It's insulting to me when I look around and see Alabama and Mississippi playing on television and Chris Schenkle comes on and makes the statement: "And these two teams epitomize the spirit of sport and fair play and brotherhood in America."

Harry Edwards, from National Educational Television's film, *Take Me Out of the Ball Game.*

9

The Battle Over Racism

Racism is everywhere in America—in the streets, in the factories, in schools, on the media, everywhere. If it is closer to the surface in sports, this may be because the sexual anxieties that provide so much of the motive force for racism are closely related to the cult of masculinity and machismo which permeates the sports world. (The argument goes that the black man must be kept in his place—otherwise he'll be after "our" women. And by this standard the black athlete, being a potential black "Superman," must be even more carefully watched and kept in his place. Hence—the exaggerated racism of the sports world.)

The racial stereotype has been, for some time, that the black is a good athlete. Today, with more and more black faces turning up on college and professional teams, it is hard for many people to imagine that these blacks are being discriminated against. But what we forget is that almost every new group of immigrants that came to America (and found itself stuck in urban ghettos and excluded from jobs) predominated in professional sports for a time. This being one of their few outlets, they had to. But this does not mean the athletes themselves weren't exploited financially by ruthless promoters and owners. Nor does it mean that they were allowed their full share of human dignity simply because they became athletic performers. This was as true of the "brawling Irish" of John L. Sullivan's day as the black athletes of today. But the race problem in sports is further complicated by the institutionalizing of racial prejudice in Western society generally that dates from a colonization of Africa at least four centuries old.

We have previously seen how the all-white character of our team sports as they developed in nineteenth-century England was intimately related to the main function of these schools and their sports—to knit together an imperialist elite which would rule over workers at home and men of color abroad. Obviously you could not have blacks in these schools or in these sports at that point because they couldn't become part of the elite. So racism in sports—as with racism generally—was part and parcel of imperialism against men of color abroad. (Much later on when it became fashionable—and absolutely necessary—to have a black puppet elite to help run the colonies, it became permissible for chiefs' sons to study at English universities and play ball with their white collaborators.) Sports was part of the system of ruling-class identification. Ruling-class people played ruling-class sports. (Soccer was finally appropriated by the English working class after a struggle lasting around six centuries—for a great deal of this time there were royal edicts against serfs kicking a ball around or taking part in games.) And, similarly in America, right down to the early fifties (and—in many sports, many schools and many parts of the country—right down until *today*) the policy of racial apartheid in sports reigns supreme, as part and parcel of the mechanisms by which white supremacy is enforced in society generally. "The essential attitude," writes Jack Olsen in *The Black Athlete: A Shameful Story* (New York: Time-Life Books, 1968), "is that these are white men's games, as indeed they are." He notes that all the blacks playing football when Paul Robeson was smashing through the line at Rutgers would not have been enough to fill a "colored only" waiting room in a small hick town in Georgia. Until less than twenty years ago, blacks who wanted to play "professional basketball" had only the option of being professional clowns (in red, white, and blue uniforms) with the Harlem Globetrotters.

At first the lack of black athletes in many sports (from which they were excluded) was pointed to as clear evidence of their "inherent inferiority." But even when blacks began to dominate certain sports like track and field, they fared no better. For example USC track coach Dean Cromwell wrote, ". . . the Negro excels in the events he does because he is closer to the primitive than the white man. It was not long ago that his ability to sprint and jump was a life-and-death matter to him in the jungle." (*Championship Technique in Track and Field,* New York: McGraw-Hill, 1941, p. 6.) In a racist society, the black man is damned if he wins, and damned if he loses. The game is rigged against him. If today we can no longer exclude the black man from "white" sports entirely, then we introduce him into them in a gradualistic and token fashion, with appropriate quotas to protect team popularity. (In a racist society it's difficult to have too many blacks on the first team—the audience might be offended.) At any rate, you can pretty much keep him out of the "thinking" positions—football quarterback, middle linebacker, center and guards, as well as coaching and managerial jobs. "The Negro may be permitted to help out," adds Jack Olsen (op. cit.), "but his role is clearly defined: he is a hired performer, and he has a job only so long as he knows his place in the white game and stays in it."

How many black referees, umpires, judges, and linesmen have you seen in professional sports? In bigtime college sports? How many black announcers? (A recent token has been the creation of what amounts to an "assistant announcer" post for blacks. It is a sad thing to see a Bill Russell acting as back-up to a white announcer who knows many a tenth as much about basketball as he does.) How many black members on the United States Olympic Committee? (That brotherhood-serving body.) On the board of the New York Athletic Club? How many black sports owners?

In one generation the situation has gone from one of virtual exclusion of blacks from American sports to what is today sometimes called the "plantation system." The contemporary situation resembles a plantation in that almost all of the overseers are white (except for the now-standard black *assistant* coach in basketball) and almost all of the top players are black. Moreover, when the professional basketball playoff games roll into town, we are faced with the odd situation of predominantly black teams playing before predominantly white suburbanite audiences. (It is again highly reminiscent of the Roman amphitheater gladiator contests in which African and Greek slaves performed for the predominantly Roman audiences.)

Even today you can pretty well keep blacks out of the elite sports—like tennis or golf or polo or even ice hockey. And if you have to have them, you have them room separately from the whites. You discourage inter-racial dating. (It's bad for the image.) And perhaps most of all you have to crush quickly the "uppity" blacks—otherwise they will all be getting out of hand.

Jack Johnson was an "uppity nigger." Worse still, he was heavyweight champ, could beat the pants off of any white around, and laugh in their face to boot. He fucked white women. So they caught him taking a white girl across state lines, and hit him with a criminal conviction for supposedly transporting her for purposes of prostitution. He was forced into exile, stripped of his title, and eventually, he claims in his autobiography, he had to make a deal to take a dive in exchange for a reduction on his jail sentence. His story is told in the play and movie *The Great White Hope*. (The title speaks for itself.)

Muhammed Ali is another "uppity" one. First he offended the white racist sportswriters by having too much to say, by not showing proper respect. He kept saying, "I am the greatest," he announced he was a black nationalist, and to top it off he changed his name (to this day the most racist sportswriters refuse to call him by his Muslim name). But his supreme heresies were to call America a racist country and to refuse to be drafted to kill other men of color in Vietnam. Obviously, he did not know his place. So just as soon as he refused to be drafted, and long before his case was decided in the courts—he was eventually acquitted— the self-appointed crusaders for Truth, Justice and the American Way on the boxing commissions decided that "Clay" was guilty until proven innocent, stripped him of his heavyweight title and refused to allow him to fight for three and half years. (By comparison, recent boxing champions adjudged as "fit" to hold their titles included professional union-buster and assaulter Sonny Liston, convicted mugger Joey Giardello, panderer Jake LaMotta, army deserter Rocky Graziano, and as a "fit" top challenger—felony murderer Ruben Carter!) The sportswriters jumped in gleefully, landing cheap shots left and right (mostly Right). The New York *Daily News*'s patriotic columnist Gene Ward contrasted Ali with Joe Louis, the latter a credit to his race and

one who dearly loved his country. Ali was not the first
uppity black to get the can. But the thing they never
have, and never can, forgive him for is that he fought
back.

Just before the 1968 Olympics, Professor Harry Edwards tried to organize an Afro-American boycott of the
Games on the grounds that their participation would be
used to bolster America's image abroad while they continued to be treated like second-class citizens at home.
One of those to join the boycott was basketball's most
outstanding player, Lew Alcindor. He was interviewed
on television by that patriotic sportscaster Joe Garagiola. With his usual bluntness Joe told this uppity black
man that, if he didn't like things in this country, he
could just get out.

Meanwhile, the Olympic establishment was having a
fit over the boycott. After all, they were fighting hard
to keep white racist Rhodesia and South Africa in the
competition. And they had been threatened with a boycott of black African and east European countries if
they did that. So eventually they had to drop their
South Africa cronies just to keep the show on the road.
Luckily for them, the black American boycott waned.
But then when sprint champions Tommy Smith and
John Carlos gave their famous black power salute during the playing at the United States National Anthem,
the Olympics establishment screamed bloody murder
that the blacks were "injecting politics into sport" (i.e.,
opposing the white supremacist politics of their bosses)
and ejected them from the Games. After some stiff
questioning from a *Ramparts* reporter at a subsequent
press conference, the U. S. Olympic Committee's press
officer demanded to see the reporter's credentials.
"You're on the nigger side, aren't you?" he said. Most
American and British sportswriters wrote that Smith
and Carlos had been soundly booed. In fact, according
to *Ramparts* sports editor Jack Scott who was there,

virtually the only boos to be heard came from these same writers! Also, although the Western media did their damndest to minimize the fact, a good many *white* Olympians stood solidly with the blacks. American hammer-throwers Hal Connolly and Ed Burke joined with various blacks on the U.S. team in threatening to withdraw from the Games after the Smith-Carlos suspensions (Scott, op. cit., p. 87). Martin Jellinghaus, wearing the button of Harry Edwards' Olympic Project for Human Rights, noted after his team's bronze finish in the 1,600-meter relay, "I am wearing this medal because I feel solidarity not only for them as persons, but for the movement, the human rights movement." Peter Norman, the Australian sprinter who shared the victory stand with Smith and Carlos and fully supported their gesture, likewise appeared wearing the Human Rights medal (and was sternly reprimanded by the Australian sports establishment). The Harvard crew team likewise supported Harry Edwards' boycott movement almost every step of the way and was repeatedly harassed by U.S. sports officials. So at least some of the white sportsmen were waking up to the way the Establishment uses racism as a weapon to divide and conquer.

It is interesting to review the records of some of the men who accused the blacks of playing politics. Once before these men had been confronted with a boycott threat. The incident is described by Richard D. Mandell in his book on *The Nazi Olympics* in Berlin in 1936. At that time the issue was that Hitler's German team discriminated against Jews. The Olympic establishment repeatedly claimed that this wasn't so, or if it was, it was irrelevant. Eventually, as the movement to boycott the Olympics gathered momentum in America, they sent General Charles Sherrill (a member of the American and International Olympic committees) to Berlin to negotiate with the Nazis. Sherrill vigorously opposed the boycott and, upon his return, discussed the reasons for his mission:

I went to Germany for the purpose of getting at least
one Jew on the German Olympic team and I feel
that my job is finished. As for obstacles placed in
the way of Jewish athletes or any others in trying to
reach Olympic ability, I would have no more business discussing that in Germany than if the Germans
attempted to discuss the Negro situation in the
American South or the treatment of the Japanese in
California. (New York *Times*, October 22, 1935.)

He also claimed that he knew many Jews who opposed
a boycott and who feared that "it would be overplaying
the Jewish hand in America as it was overplayed in
Germany before the present suppression and expulsion
of the Jews were undertaken." The next day, Frederick
Rubin, then Secretary of the American Olympic Committee announced his position: "Germans are not dis-
criminating against Jews in their Olympic tryouts. The
Jews are eliminated because they are not good enough
as athletes. Why there are not a dozen Jews in the
world of Olympic caliber." (New York *Times*, October
23, 1935.) General Sherrill later appeared before the
Italian Chamber of Commerce in New York and praised
Mussolini as "a man of courage in a world of pussyfoot-
ers," adding, "I wish to God he'd come over here and
have a chance to do that same thing." (New York
Times, November 27, 1935.)

The President of the American Olympic Committee
(and close colleague of Sherrill and Rubin) was Avery
Brundage. He has remained at the top of the Olympic
establishment ever since, and is presently head of the
International Olympic Committee. He opposed the
anti-Nazi boycott just as he was later to oppose the
black boycott. He opposed exclusion of Germany in
1936, of Japan in 1940, and of Rhodesia and South Africa in 1968. In 1936, according to Mandell, "Brundage
and his supporters posed as being far above petty
chauvinism—a position that did not prevent them from

occasionally praising the visible accomplishments of the Nazis and from slurring the adherents of (the boycott) Committee on Fair Play as being Reds or even Communists."

In May 1968 *Ramparts* reported that Brundage had told an AAU National Convention that the German Jews were "satisfied" with their treatment under the Nazis. Was this just a hastily thought-out view based largely on ignorance? Apparently not. For even after Brundage made the trip to Nazi Germany with the 1936 American Olympic team, he returned to a packed rally of 20,000 at Madison Square Garden with heady praise for the Nazi establishment. According to the October 3, 1936, New York *Times*, Avery Brundage "brought his audience to their feet cheering in an outburst of enthusiasm when he paid tribute to the Reich under Adolf Hitler." He told them, "We can learn much from Germany. We, too, if we wish to preserve our institutions, must stamp out communism. We, too, must take steps to arrest the decline of patriotism."

"As recently as August 1940," *Ramparts* reported, "Brundage was serving as head of Citizens to Keep America Out of War, a group now known to have been Nazi-supported." It came as no great surprise that the only two Jews on the American track and field team, Sam Stoller and Marty Glickman, were mysteriously dropped from the 400-meter relay team just before the start of the Berlin Games.

Whenever college athletes become "rebellious"—and even more especially whenever *black* college athletes become rebellious—some coach or sportswriter will inevitably come out with the old garbage about how "the college has given these athletes a free education for which they should be grateful." The argument goes that the sports teams were the first things on campus to be integrated, and "if it wasn't for sports they'd still be back in their ghettos." (This is like a boss who tells his striking employee, "if it wasn't for me you wouldn't have a job.") First of all, is it not curious that the first college sport to be "integrated," namely football, is also the sport that makes the most money? Is it not curious that the "integration" of college basketball, especially at some of the Big Ten schools, has come along only in the last decade? That college baseball is still 98 per cent lily white? That schools such as the University of Texas at El Paso which were eager to welcome black athletic crowd-pleasers onto their campus with open arms took quite awhile to extend the same admission to non-athletic black students? "The black athlete in the predominantly white school," says Harry Edwards in *The Revolt of the Black Athlete* (New York: Free Press, 1969), "was and is first, foremost, and sometimes only, an athletic commodity." But, you say, at least he gets an education. Yes, an "education" composed mostly of courses in things like phys ed and basket weaving. He's expected to give most of his time to the "team." And after his athletic eligibility ends, so does his scholarship. Most never even graduate. They end up right back in the ghetto.

Lately, with the exception of the lily-white teams of the deep South, as more and more black faces are seen on the playing fields, some white sports fans have been getting more and more impatient. During the 1969 Notre Dame-Michigan State basketball game at South Bend, the Notre Dame coach committed the extreme *faux pas* of having five black faces on the court at the same time. Never mind that they were his best players. The overwhelmingly white "Fighting Irish" student body at Notre Dame field house nearly had a fit. Hoots and boos rang through to the rafters whenever the five black players were on the court together. The black players resigned and did not rejoin the team till they received a public apology from the president of the Notre Dame student body. The mask of white liberal-ism was wearing very thin, and the racism was increasingly showing through. A few years earlier, Dick Harp, the basketball coach at Kansas had resigned in disgust at the abuse he had received from fans and alumni for starting four black players during the 1963–64 season.

No doubt the exploitation of the white athlete is almost equally ruthless. He too gets his share of junk courses. Gives his all for the team, while the college collects the profits. He, too, a large part of the time never graduates. But he also has a lot of job opportunities that his black teammate does not. He has not been so thoroughly coaxed into believing that sports is his best chance to "make it" in life. Jack Olsen points out that although sports has led a few thousand blacks out of the ghetto, for hundreds of thousands—maybe millions—of others, "it has substituted a meaningless dream. It has helped to perpetuate an oppressive system." Though sports may also have provided an arena in which blacks vicariously acted out their aggressions against whites by cheering on their heroes, it did little to deal with the grievances that caused such aggressions. Hence, even integrated sports have been used as a racial opiate.

At times the use of black athletes in college sports resembles nothing so much as a modern version of the slave trade, in which coaches send their scouts out looking for quality black horse flesh to reel in the trophies (and the cash), only to be thrown back in their ghetto cages when the game ends. "The whites call the Negro football players cannibals," said UTEP (University of Texas at El Paso) basketballer Willie Worsley, "and the basketball players [who in 1966 won the NCAA Championship] animals. You play basketball and that's it. When the game's over they want you to come back to the dormitory and stay out of sight." His athletic director George McCarty replies, "Four of our colored alumni are playing pro basketball right now . . . and you can't just say that we got a bunch of cattle in here and milked them. It was profitable both ways." And who says they aren't still being "milked" in the pros? "You know those junkyards along the highways in Jersey?" says former Cleveland Indians outfielder Larry Doby, who was the first black to be allowed into the American League. "Well, they have scrap heaps just like that for athletes—most of them black. Black athletes are cattle. They're raised, fed, sold and killed . . . Baseball moved me toward the front of the bus, and it let me ride there as long as I could run. And then it told me to get off at the back door." (Jack Olsen, op. cit.) "They look upon us as nothing but animals," said Olympic sprinter John Carlos. "Low animals, roaches, and ants . . . They give us peanuts, pat us on the back and say, 'Boy, you did fine.'" Behind all the outrage that blacks are not more grateful for "the chances we've given them" lies the old apartheid attitude that, after all, blacks don't really belong on "our" sports fields and colleges; they are only there because we "gave" them something. As if anything that great were happening on the football fields and colleges! The main thing happening in football is that a lot of guys are being injured so that others can make big profits. As for the colleges, the main things they are teaching are the top-down view of the world, contempt for all those not in college, and absolute obedience to the administration. (Happily, many students have other ideas.)

But times are changing, and black athletes are getting the message. In 1965 black members of the American Football League All-Star teams banded together and refused to play the game in racially biased New Orleans, Louisiana. The AFL's Commissioner had to move the game to another city. (Unfortunately, as a direct result of this incident, the AFL's two top black running backs, Abner Haynes and Cookie Gilchrist, were promptly traded and were soon seen riding the bench on their new teams.)

Two years later the season's opening football game between San Jose State College and UTEP had to be cancelled when black San Jose student activists threatened they would break it up as a protest against racism on their campus. (There were also rumors that if the game were played, SJS's stadium would be "burned to the ground.") November 1967 brought the start of the Olympic boycott campaign. It was strongly supported by Lew Alcindor:

> Everybody knows me. I'm the big basketball star, the weekend hero, everybody's All-American. Well, last summer I was almost killed by a racist cop shooting at a black cat in Harlem. He was shooting on the street—where masses of black people were standing around or just taking a walk. But he didn't care. After all we were just niggers ["Doc" Ellis and Willis Reed would have similar experiences.] . . . Somewhere each of us has got to make a stand against this kind of thing. (Harry Edwards, op. cit.)

February 1968 brought a black boycott of the New York Athletic Club's games in protest against the club's membership bar against blacks:

> The intransigence of the N.Y.A.C. in its refusal to even admit the problem of racism in its ranks, much less take steps to rectify it, is, we believe, indicative of the present demeanor of White America toward taking real steps to deal with racism in this society. We see, through this protest, that it isn't just racist *individuals* we are up against. It's a racist conspiracy involving many of the would-be-great institutions of the Society. (From the boycotters' press release.)

The same month black athletes at the University of California's Berkeley campus threatened to boycott, picket, and disrupt all the school's athletic competitions unless the athletic director and the basketball coach

were replaced, black coaches were hired, more black
students were recruited, more black studies courses included in the curriculum, and the treatment of blacks
on campus was greatly improved. They won all of their
demands including the replacement of the athletic
director and football coach. (Similar boycott threats
or protests were made at, among other places, Michigan
State University, Western Michigan University,
Marquette, Kansas, San Francisco State, Washington, and Princeton. (Some token Negro coaches were
promptly hired to cool things down.) All in all, there
were racial revolts on the teams of no less than thirty-
seven major college campuses in the year 1967–68
alone.

There were also serious racial flare-ups on the St.
Louis Cardinals and Cleveland Browns pro football
teams. In St. Louis a lot of the dissension was caused by
the attitude of white players and coaches toward interracial dating. "They won't have our respect," one
white Cardinal said about his black teammates, "as long
as they keep getting caught with white women. To me
that's the worst offense there is—dating white girls."
Roy Shivers tells about the time he ran into the fiancée
of a white friend from his college days. A couple of
Cardinal coaches promptly came up "and gave us the
funny look." Then there was some advice from an older
Negro player: "The coach wants you to cool it, be a
bit more discreet." According to running back Johnny
Roland, the coaches "set a tone that the white racist
guys just follow. Some of the coaches treat us like animals, so why shouldn't the players do the same." Bernie
Parrish writes that to Cincinnati Bengals and former
Cleveland Browns head coach Paul Brown the players
were just his "animals." "When Jim Brown ripped off a
good gain or two early in a game," says Parrish, "Paul
would rub his hands together and whisper to John
Wooten, one of his messenger guards [and black], 'The
animal's runnin' today—the animal's ready today.'"

(Parrish, op. cit., pp. 95–96.) And Paul Brown was no fly-by-night fill-in coach. For more than twenty-five years he has been at the very top of the professional football coaching profession. Similarly, with Alvin Dark. It's now about ten years since he made his famous remarks about black and Latin American baseball players being not as bright as whites, lazy and lacking in team spirit to boot. Although Dark was fired that year (for getting on the wrong side of his owner) he returned to the majors and soon had one of the longest managerial careers in baseball.

"There are definite signs of quotas and definite signs that black players are stacked at certain positions," continued the Cardinals' Johnny Roland. "It isn't enough for a Negro to be good to make this team. He's got to be better than good." Similarly in baseball.[1] Aaron Rosenblatt's statistical survey in *Trans-Action* showed that in the seasons 1962–65 inclusive, the average black major leaguer hit 21.2 points higher than the average white, and that approximately the same percentage held for the preceding nine years.

"It's a sad thing to face," said Cardinal fullback Prentice Gautt, "but racial prejudice is almost a tradition in sports." He remarks that black athletes could be telling other blacks that there is no need to rebel. "But what kind of hypocrites would we be to go back

[1] It is also worth noting that except for a few outstanding players there have been very few Jewish major leaguers. Dave Oliphant, a Connecticut businessman formerly the property of the New York Yankees, gave Curt Flood some clues as to why. He was sent to a farm club "whose manager, a rabid anti-Semite ostracized him—except when threatening to get rid of 'that Jewboy.'" He eventually asked for his release; but to get it, his father had to *buy* back his contract. With things like this going on, it's disgusting to see blacks and Jews in places like New York fighting each other for crumbs, while the racists who are screwing them both get the cake. (*The Way It Is,* p. 199.)

and tell them a better day is coming, when that day isn't even in sight on the playing field?"

Carl Brettschneider, a former player and front-office man with the Detroit Lions told Bernie Parrish, "The Lions, while I was personnel director, they practically ordered me to draft more colored guys than white guys. You know why? Cheaper, they sign cheaper." When Parrish asked him if it was correct that black players are paid less than white players of comparable ability, he replied, "Oh, I think so, sure, sure." (Parrish, op. cit., pp. 149–50.)

In his autobiography, *Confessions of a Dirty Ballplayer* (New York: Dell, 1971, p. 85), Johnny Sample tells the story of the problems he had getting a just raise after he first made All-Pro cornerback. "I know you had a great year, Sample," said his coach. "But black athletes just don't deserve that kind of money and I won't pay it." (The coach in question had his personal elderly black valet "Bootsy," who would wake him up in the morning, spit polish his shoes, get him his coffee, etc., "for which he was paid next to nothing and treated like a dog.") In 1963, John Nisby of the Redskins and John Henry Johnson the top fullback for the Steelers started writing a book on racism in the NFL. They wrote to every black player in the league for information. According to Sample, Chicago Bears owner-coach George Halas somehow got a copy, called up all the other owners "and all hell broke loose." Sample says, "John Nisby was quickly ousted." (Ibid., pp. 214–15.) Johnson was one of the top rushers in the league; so he was allowed to stay for a while. But in 1965 he injured his leg and got the heave-ho. "This kind of thing will continue," says Sample, "until black players get together and put a stop to it."

Parrish gives another interesting example. Clifton McNeil, the wide receiver who led the NFL in pass receiving with seventy-one catches in 1968, had the boldness to insist on a substantial raise for his successes.

Not only was it refused, but according to Parrish, "he was disciplined for having the temerity to ask by being benched through most of the next season . . . and at the end of the year he was traded to the Giants as damaged goods." (Parrish, op. cit., p. 152.) He managed to catch fifty passes for the Giants in 1970, but early the following year he was suddenly shipped to the Redskins.

Walter Roberts, one of the Redskins' outstanding flankers of 1970, had previously gone to New Orleans in the expansion draft. "After one season," writes Parrish, "Tom Fears [the New Orleans coach] suspected Walt of organizing the black players, so he made a deal with Detroit to take Roberts for a little while, then drop him and blackball him from the league." (Ibid., p. 179.) Walt Roberts had to sit out of pro football for a year. Bob Brown, an All-Pro offensive tackle with the Los Angeles Rams was suddenly shipped to the Oakland Raiders. "You've really got trouble there," the San Francisco *Chronicle* says the Raiders' general manager was told. "It's funny," said Brown much later. "If you speak up for your rights, you're a troublemaker, and if you're a black athlete who speaks up, you're really bad." All-Pro tight end John Mackey had the reputation of being a fairly mild fellow until he took over as president of the NFL Players' Association and led them through the 1970 strike. After that he was often referred to as a "Bolshevik." A year later he found himself playing second string. "You have to have the right 'attitude' or you can't play," noted Baltimore Colts All-Pro tackle Jim Parker. "At Ohio State I had a friend who I thought could play a good game, but the coach said he didn't have the right [Right?] 'attitude,' so he sat on the bench for four years. Even in pro football you look at a guy and you think he can play, and then one day he's on the train going home; something to do with his 'attitude.' You worry about it, but you don't

ask any questions because you have a family to feed."
(Olsen, op. cit.)

During the 1970 college football season at least
seventy-nine black athletes boycotted or were suspended from their teams over charges of racism. Possibly the most serious flare-up was at Syracuse University where eight blacks boycotted the squad and
two more dropped off for "medical" reasons.

Ben Schwartzwalder, the Syracuse coach, is probably
one of the best known and most successful coaches in
college sports. He has won bowl games, been named
"Coach of the Year," and has had top black players like
Jimmy Brown, Floyd Little, and the late Ernie Davis.

As the 1969–70 academic year drew to a close, racial
tensions on the Syracuse football squad headed toward
the boiling point. It was said that black players had
been addressed by coaches as "Hey, boy!" and
"nigger." That blacks, such as Richie Bulls, had received tongue lashings for being seen around with
white girls. That coach Schwartzwalder seemed un-
duly keen about blacks shaving off their mustaches.
Afro hair styles were absolutely taboo. Later, at a
basketball game at the Syracuse field house, the coach
jumped hard on blacks who refused to stand for the
National Anthem:

> With all the crap we were going through at the
> school, and with this country fostering apartheid here
> and in South Africa, killing Asians who are Black,
> adding to the oppression of Arabs in the Middle East,
> I didn't think that I should stand and salute a flag of
> a country that is not mine. The United States has
> never taken into account the welfare of Blacks in any
> of its economic policies. In fact they foster unemploy-
> ment among Blacks as a tool to fight inflation. They
> keep Blacks in a poverty spectrum. Why should I
> stand and recognize this flag? (Defensive back
> Duane Walker, quoted in *Black Sports*, June 1971.)

Schwartzwalder told them he didn't want any "commies" on his team. They would either stand for the Anthem or get out. (Eventually black players would stay in their locker rooms during the playing of the Anthem.)

Then there were the hundred and one intangible things that convinced the black athletes that the coaches and the school regarded them as "super-niggers," good enough to beat their brains in on the field for the Ole Alma Mater, but not much good for anything else. They decided that they wanted a black coach—he at least might have some understanding about their grievances—and put their point of view to the head coach. After the university came up with nothing, the players suggested that a black professional be hired to stick with the squad for the thirty-day 1970 spring training session. The coaches eventually came up with Floyd Little, the Denver Broncos pro who, in his days at Syracuse, had bitterly opposed a petition from other black athletes against games with schools with proven records of racial discrimination. According to linebacker Jeff Logan, Little's participation in spring training consisted of little more than walking out onto the field for an hour one day, and then disappearing. The black players figured they had been had (*Black Sports,* June 1971).

The fourth day of spring training they boycotted practice. They were immediately suspended, and even threatened with being kicked off campus (though, as the publicity glare flooded the university, they were eventually allowed to stay). When the administration suggested that the suspensions be lifted, the white jocks unanimously voted against it. (A year earlier when the blacks had first asked for a black coach, the whites had unanimously voted that they would not play for one.)

Nothing could have shown more clearly the ability of the system to use racism to divide the people against each other. One of the blacks' main complaints had

been inferior medical attention—being sent back onto
the field to risk permanent disability when you were
really too injured to play. "I've got calcium deposits in
my knee," declared one white jock, "but that's my
problem. I'm not going to complain about it." Then,
too, not only had coaches called some players "nigger,"
they had called others "wop," "polack," "dirty kraut,"
and so on. Most important, both white and black players had been subject to the same vicious authoritarianism. Only the whites thought that they had to take their
football complete with a dictatorship, and that was
that. The blacks were trying to do something about it.
But the whites thought that the color of their skin gave
them more in common with their bosses than it did with
their black fellows. (Of course a lot of this response
was manipulated by the coaches.)

Eventually with the football season about to get under way the Chancellor of the University appointed a
committee of trustees, administrators, professors, and
students to look into the situation:

> The Committee concludes that racism in the
> Syracuse University Athletic Department is real,
> chronic, largely unintentional, and sustained and
> complicated unwittingly by many modes of behavior
> common in American athletics and longstanding at
> Syracuse University . . . The definition of the spring
> boycott merely as an issue of violating coaching au-
> thority, and the penalizing of black athletes without
> taking into consideration the broader context of their
> protest was an act of institutional racism unworthy of
> a great university. (From the Committee's Report.)

The Chancellor allowed as how he found the findings
"fair," but did nothing to discipline the coaches. The
Committee called for the suspended players to receive
an additional year of football eligibility, and for the
running of the athletic programs to be taken out of the
hands of the administration and put under the control

of a committee representing different segments of the (so-called) university community. Instead of a pledge to obey the coach—as the administration had demanded —they recommended a sort of "bill of rights" for athletes, guaranteeing them the same rights of dress, hair length, and political involvement as are allowed other students. A kind of jock liberation.

Naturally the report was, for the most part, quietly shelved. Committee reports not backed by any threat of militancy are seldom worth the paper they are written on. Indeed, a short time later some Syracuse alumni gave Schwartzwalder a testimonial dinner at the Hotel Americana, and *congratulatory* messages arrived from Governor Rockefeller and President Nixon.

Coach Jim Harding of the University of Detroit is not unlike a good many other coaches. Where he is almost unique is that in November 1970 his entire team simply refused to play for him anymore. In a letter signed by the thirteen black players and three whites who made up the varsity basketball squad, Harding was accused of "failure to recognize us as human beings with human feelings." When informed that he had a team without any players, the coach remained unperturbed. "If that's what they said," he told the wire services, "then they won't remain on the team long. *I* am the head coach and will be here for the next three years." (Face-saving gestures were made, and the players eventually returned.)

In December 1970 four blacks on the University of Washington football team turned in their cleats, charging that the racial practices of the coaches "have forced us to the point where we no longer can tolerate the playing conditions imposed upon us." Charges of racism had previously been leveled at Washington football coaches for more than two years, beginning with spring practice 1968. As at other schools, one of the main issues was interracial dating. Junior Coffey, later a fullback in the NFL (where various teams said he had a bad "attitude") suddenly found himself benched in college. When he asked his assistant coach at Washington why, he was told, "You're dating this white girl and I'd advise you not to do it. I think it would be detrimental to your future, and it could be a reflection on other Negro players." He says it was even hinted that the University would stop recruiting black athletes altogether if he did not knuckle under. At the time Junior Coffey was the *third leading rusher in the nation*. And he never started another Varsity game!

"It has also been discrimination," Charlie Sifford told a reporter for *Black Sports* (June 1971), "that has kept the black golfer ten to fifteen years behind." And yet, we are supposed to weep huge tears when blacks protest the appearance of South Africa's Gary Player at tournaments like the Master's that most black Americans still don't get into. But the anti-apartheid forces are not exactly taking it lying down. In addition to the welcomes for Gary Player, there were disruptions of the games of the South African Springboks cricket and rugby tours in Britain, Ireland, Australia, and New Zealand. (The cricket tour had to be cancelled in Britain because, it was said, black nationalists were "using" the issue to set back race relations some twenty years. Presumably they threatened to have more *equal* race relations.) Nor have South African tennis players been ignored. There have been sit-ins on the courts, hecklings, even aerial bombardments. And in British swimming, Olympic team captain Tony Jarvis greeted the appearance of Prime Minister Edward Heath at the 1970 Commonwealth Games by brandishing a placard proclaiming: "Heath. South African Arms Dealer." In the most faithful traditions of British racist sports, Jarvis was threatened with debarment from the European championships and forced to sign a "no politics" pledge.

In recent years there has also been a growing chorus

of protest about the racist stereotypes of American Indians encouraged by the names and emblems of many American professional teams. Names like the Redskins, Indians, Braves and so on—often with emblems showing a hook-nosed, racist stereotype of an Indian —have come under increasing attack both in the United States and Canada.

At the Oakland Coliseum Arena, meanwhile, pentathlon star Sam Goldberg was back in competition. A year earlier he was kicked off the track team at the University of Kansas and lost his scholarship, after he announced that he was dedicating a victory medal to the Black Panthers. He finished a close second in the Oakland meet to the 1970 AAU decathalon champion and beat out a member of the U. S. Olympic team. "I'm dedicating the medal I won tonight," said the blond-haired Goldberg, "to Bobby Seale." He said he was running for an organization whose existence the AAU would rather not face up to—Woodstock International:

> The idea behind Woodstock is a combination of the Black Panther Party's concept of community involvement, and that of progressive working class—in short, it's sports for the people. Let's face it, man. Because of the conservative element in our society, sports have become political. We're competing for the flag, the country, and everything else. My event, without going on an ego trip of what I've done, is for the people. My participation, and everyone competing for Woodstock, is dedicated to America's getting out of Vietnam and the Black Panther Party and anyone else that's getting ripped off.

He added that, when he runs in the big meets, he wears high top gym shoes, "like the brothers in the ghetto, because like them I can't afford those twenty-dollar jogger shoes." (*San Francisco Examiner,* February 13, 1971.)

We recognize our old friend, our old mole, who knows *so* well how to work underground, suddenly to appear: THE REVOLUTION!

Marx

10

Cultural Revolution--
Socialism or Fascism?

When the fighters no longer fight, and the scorers no longer score, the empire starts cracking apart at the seams. The natives in the neo-colonies are restless. Rebellions break out. Vietnam leads the way. At home, workers' strikes, student occupations, black uprisings, women's lib, repression. Babylon is trembling. "In the sports world, as in society at large," writes Jack Scott in *The Athletic Revolution,* "individuals representing an authoritarian, anti-life force are lining up in opposition to those representing a creative, humanistic life force."

Sport psychologists Bruce Ogilvie and Thomas Tutko (who are certainly no foes of the athletic establishment) have acknowleged that after extensively testing coaches throughout the United States, they have found them to be one of—if not *the*—most authoritarian groups of individuals in American society. As for their attitudes on racial questions, Scott recalls the remarks of one of his own college coaches, who used to lecture his white jocks on the "good feeling" they should get whenever they "beat a nigger." The rash of racial uprisings in college athletic departments would seem to indicate that these sentiments are anything but untypical of the coaching fraternity. Nor was the response of the NCAA's athletic establishment anything but typical. Instead of doing anything about racism in college athletics, they moved instead to throw out any "troublemaking" athletes (and mostly black athletes at that) who might call it to their attention.[1] We are reminded of the Wyoming football coach who sacked over a dozen black players from his team simply because they wore black arm bands as a gesture in protest against having to play Brigham Young (Scott, op.

---

[1] A member institution may terminate the financial aid of a student-athlete if he is adjudged to have been guilty of manifest disobedience through violation of institutional regulations or established athletic department policies and rules applicable to all student athletes. Construed to be manifest disobedience are disruptive actions which interfere with the normal and orderly conduct of an institution's athletic program, refusal to meet the normal good-conduct obligations required of all team members and defiance of the normal and necessary directions of the departmental staff members. (A resolution passed at the 1969 NCAA Convention.)

We might add that in the same year a very similar proposal to suspend the grants of rebellious British students was hooted down as fascistic by the majority of the British national newspapers. In the NCAA case, what debate there was on the motion indicated that "disruptive action" included especially such things as the Smith-Carlos Black Power salute in Mexico and the 1968 University of Texas at El Paso track boycott. A storm of controversy also broke out about whether an athlete could be stripped of his scholarship for refusing to have a haircut!

cit., p. 133). Jack Scott says that a nationally prominent
track coach told him, "Unless we can find a way to separate the decent ones from the troublemakers and mili-
tants, we're going to stop recruiting all Negroes." Scott
adds that, "Given their years of unquestioned authoritarian rule, coaches like Paul 'Bear' Bryant and Ben
Schwartzwalder are about as likely to begin behaving
democratically as is General Franco." (Op. cit., p. 198.)
(Scott was viciously attacked for this remark by Vice-
President Spiro Agnew, who explained to Bear Bryant's
supporters on the Touchdown Club of Birmingham,
Alabama, that, although the U.S. supported General
Franco, Scott did not mean this comparison "as a compliment.")

What it means for a football coach to behave
democratically was developed further by South Car-
olina coach Paul Dietzel. "We have a complete democracy as far as the squad is concerned," declared the
coach. "We do exactly as I want them to do, and in my
way of thinking that is complete democracy, because I
am very prejudiced." (Neil Amdur, *The Fifth Down*,
p. 30.) On January 14, 1970, Dietzel who was then
president of the American Football Coaches Association gave a speech to his fellow football führers on the
subject of hair:

> I really have never paid any attention to the idea of
> how popular I am with my squad because, frankly,
> a good bit of the time our squad hates my guts . . .
> I remember I was talking with the fellows from Ole
> Miss, and they handle it relatively the same way that
> we do. You see we tell our athletes that part of your
> training rules, and it says on our Atlantic Coast Con-
> ference Contract that the training rules shall be part
> of the things that you must live up to, to maintain
> your scholarship . . . is that you cannot wear these
> girl haircuts, because I like to make sure we are
> coaching boys, and you cannot wear sideburns down

beneath this hole in the side of your head or you have to cut those sideburns right off at that hole. If you have them any lower than that, we don't say anything, you can wear them there if you don't want to eat. But it is pretty simple, if you want to eat, you cut off your sideburns.

Well, you will be surprised how effective that has been because almost everyone wants to eat, and we have a fine training table year round. So as I say we have a complete democracy on the hair, if they want to eat, they cut their hair. And very frankly, every few months, I have to go in and slap a few wrists, they miss a few meals, they get ticked off when we will not let them eat. Eventually, their hunger and having to go down and buy hamburgers instead of eating those fine foods kind of gets to them.

"Football is not a democracy," says University of Pittsburgh grid coach Carl DePasqua. "There's nothing to debate. The players can debate in political science class." (Amdur, ibid., p. 23.) Syracuse's Ben Schwartzwalder agrees. He says that, as coach, "you look on yourself as a kind of benevolent dictator." (Ibid.) The "benevolent dictator" label (which, after all, was also a favorite with Hitler) has also been taken up with pride by Indiana grid coach John Pont, whom many sportswriters point to as a liberal coach. "It's a sad and frightening commentary on the state of intercollegiate athletics," writes Jack Scott, "when a coach like John Pont—a man who refused to allow certain black athletes even to try out for Indiana's football team simply because he did not approve of their attitude— is viewed as a liberal coach." (Op. cit., p. 199.)

Again, it must be emphasized, that all this "benevolent" authoritarianism is not just the haphazard quirks of a few oddball coaches. (We are, in any case, talking about some of the most respected and typical members of the coaching fraternity. And, if they are oddballs,

we should still have to account for the fact that these
oddballs have been placed by supposedly great universities in positions of enormous power.) As Dietzel
emphasized, most of our leading colleges and universities are now requiring athletes to sign a contract
promising, in effect, absolute obedience to the coach
before they are allowed to play. And what contracts
they are:

> The athlete must at all times be neatly attired, clean-
> shaven, well-groomed and have an acceptable hair-
> cut. (By acceptable, we mean that it must be
> acceptable to the Head Coach of the given
> sport . . .) While on or off campus, athletes are ex-
> pected to wear neat and acceptable clothing . . .
> There are to be no symbols, demonstrations or other
> displays of protest on the practice or playing areas or
> while a team is brought together for a team func-
> tion . . . The athlete will keep his shoes well
> polished . . . (From the contract at Colorado State
> University.)

And suddenly there is much worry from the coaches
and sportswriters that the athletes are becoming
"political." Back in the days when the jocks at the University of California, Columbia, and a score of other
institutions, were beating up student demonstrators,
there was no great fear that the athletes were
"political." No great speculations that their tactics
might be "neo-nazi." Jim Bouton (op. cit.) points out
that as long as professional baseball players could be
depended upon rabidly to support the Vietnam war,
the Army, General Patton, and the Flag, no one in baseball's establishment worried about what they were saying or whether it was "political." But once certain
players started disagreeing with the war, started questioning the view that the generals were always right,
the baseball brass suddenly thought that the players
were being "political."

In 1970, for the first time in history, the American

Broadcasting Company (ABC) refused to televise the half-time show of the Holy Cross-Buffalo football game because it was "political." The Buffalo marching band had scheduled simulated formations of smoking factories and exploding bombs and would play such "controversial" songs as "We Shall Overcome" and "Give Peace a Chance." A few weeks later, ABC and the NCAA proudly televised the half-time at the Army-Navy game, complete with a squad of Army Rangers who had just returned from an abortive raid on a North Vietnamese POW camp, and greetings from the Joint Chiefs of Staff. Nothing "political" about that.

Dr. Lyle Owen, professor of Economics at the University of Tulsa, wrote in the spring 1971 *American Association of University Professors Bulletin* about a monthly meeting of his chapter at which the guest of honor and speaker was the head football coach. "Football Prevents Communism," the coach declared:

> This professor of football—the coaches are all members of the faculty so that what they do may be kept noncommercial—made it a central point in his oration that no football player had ever become a Communist, therefore the sport is a prime preventive. I had not realized before, when wondering how we should grapple with Marxism-Leninism-Maoism, that football is the answer. This information alone was worth the price of my annual dues.

Jack Scott (op. cit., p. 206) points out that football coaches such as Frank Kush at Arizona State and Jim Ward, the ex-Maryland coach, have openly admitted that they hit players when they get angry. Vinnie Lombardi sometimes did it as a matter of course, just to get more out of his players. "Violent behavior by coaches—men who like to call themselves educators," says Scott, "is not at all unusual," although at most places the head coach is content to leave the cop or "enforcer" role to one of his assistants. "Violence by coaches," he adds, "is called building character, but

when student protestors use it, even liberal faculty
members castigate them by labeling their tactics neo-
nazi." (Ibid.) Nothing "neo-nazi" about the coaches, of
course.

At the height of the uproar about the suspension of
black gridders at Syracuse, the university's Chancellor
offered to reinstate them if the blacks would sign what
amounted to a "loyalty oath" promising undying
obedience to head coach Schwartzwalder. At Georgia
Tech the Deep South's first black quarterback at a
predominantly white college, Eddie McAshan, was reportedly barred from practice for criticizing his white
coach. "I have never known Eddie to be disloyal . . ."
the United Press quoted the coach. In the end, a head-
line in the Philadelphia *Bulletin* (September 29, 1971)
declared:

Black Tech QB Is Reinstated;
"Loyalty" Upheld

It is also becoming increasingly common for college
coaches to ask black athletes to sign pledges promising
that they will put their sports before anything else.
Blacks who refuse to sign this latest version of the
loyalty oaths are banned from the team. Many black
athletes believe that to sign such a pledge would be a
betrayal of the black freedom struggle, and they are
refusing to do it.

You really have to wonder how such hyperirrever-
ent non-conformists as Babe Ruth and Ty Cobb would
have fared in today's fascistic sports atmosphere. No
doubt they'd have the makings to be stars in any case.
But would they be given the chance? Alex Johnson was
the best hitter in the American League. And Duane
Thomas was just about the best runner in the National
Football League. But, when they started getting a bit
uppity, they were quickly given the bum's rush. (Also,
they are black.) If they had spoken out the way they
did in high school or college in the present environment,

it is likely that no one would ever have heard of them, regardless of their talent.

To give the coaches their due, it must be admitted that there is a distinctly Right-wing flare in many a football fan's eye. (And we have talked a bit about the socializing mechanisms in sports that put it there.) College football has always thrived most in the Southeast, Southwest and Midwest; in short, in what might be called the more tradition-minded sections of the country. But the connection between college football, tradition, and myths of college or national greatness was not something invented by Right-wing fanatics. Rather, it was something created and nurtured along every step of the way by the administrators and top alumni of many of America's leading universities. Basically, the idea was that if you could get the old grads to come back for the Big Games, perfume them a bit with the fragrance of college tradition and all that, you would be much more likely to get contributions to the college building fund. If some of the alumni were organized in a fraternity or a military unit (a college ROTC group, for example), it was just that much easier to get them to come out together. And so what if you threw in a little patriotism with the half-time show. College nationalism is just one of the socializing units for American nationalism; for Americanism. The idea is that if the students could be steered to identify with their college and its traditions, it would be that much easier to identify with the country and its (properly whitewashed) traditions. And vice versa. If you could convince the old grads that college football, and college tradition generally, was Americanism, then the building fund was sure to boom.

A large part of the traditions that made that Big Game so big had to do with repressed sexuality. The Big Games, Winter Weekend, and particularly Homecoming Weekend, were the officially recognized occasions when our sexually repressed collegians and alumni of former generations got together to blow off a little steam. Alcohol flowed freely at the parties. Maybe you even brought a flask to the game. Like New Year's Eve, this was one of the few festive occasions when the barriers of sexual repression came down. Sex was O.K. if enjoyed in the proper spirit: combined with alcohol; fraternity parties; spending money. And the whole thing was sold to the old grads as something called "tradition." It was, and is, a big seller.

Having a winning team was important to the ritual. It provided just that much more reason to celebrate— and to contribute to the building fund. Wealthy alumni, preselected through such traditions, were willing to make all sorts of under-the-table payments to help build a winning team. For them—and Vinnie Lombardi became their prophet—winning was the *only* thing. In the later part of the '6os, however, with student rebellions breaking out on one college campus after another, it quickly became evident to college administrators that many of these wealthy alumni would rather have a *losing* team composed entirely of crew-cut, sexually repressed flag-wavers than one that included any long-haired potential anti-war demonstrators or black nationalists. Football's role as a money maker through ticket sales was declining relative to its role as an advertising, socializing, and public relations medium. So, in these militarized times, the emphasis on winning gradually had to take second place to the one on conformity. Everyone knew that the really Big Game was the one being fought in southeast Asia. The long and the short of the matter, in the past few years, is that even at home the society is quite literally in a state of civil war. University administrations against their students. Short hair against long. Factory bosses against their workers. Increasingly, it is fascism against socialism. With this kind of conflict shaping up, any manifestation of free thinking or independence, even the mildest criticism of one's superiors, is regarded as "disloyalty," and punishable as treason.

In a way it is unfortunate that I have been using such

static terms as "jock" and "fan" to refer to well-socialized players and spectators. The truth is that no one is born a sexist, an elitist, or a racist. These qualities have to be socialized into them by the kind of system that has distinct uses for fascist character structures (and it may be largely eliminated by love, interhuman solidarity, and struggle against that system). The groundwork is laid in childhood, where the regime of vicious sexual repression, sado-masochism, love-hate for authority, and the distorted Oedipal conception of the American nuclear family begins. Sexism flows naturally from sexual repression. Competitiveness from inter-sibling rivalries for the limited affection of only two adults (in fact, usually only the mother is available). Love and approval are turned into weapons, given or withheld depending on the degree of performance and respect for authority. And the teacher and the coach take up from where the parents have left off. With outlets for genuine sexual or vocational fulfillment in short supply, status—and especially the pseudo status of sports and fraternities—becomes the order of the day. Under the stern eyes of authoritarian and sexually repressive coaches, the socialization in sexism and authoritarianism can continue in earnest. The pseudo elitism of the varsity jock is the prize. The winners are given the pick of the strenuously limited cosmetic sexual opportunities, the highest pseudo status, and special license to act like drunken sadistic buffoons. In his book *High for the Game* (p. 115), former Oakland Raiders and University of Southern California line-backer Chip Oliver tells how in his college days he came to be known as "Rude Ralph," famous for his lewd remarks and off-color behavior around girls. But he was a rough-and-ready footballer, and this was the sort of behavior the fans expected.

In the society governed by the so-called Reality Principle of vicious sexual repression—or, what is the same thing, repressive cosmetics-and-commodity sexual pseudo fulfillment—fascism seems still capable of

galvanizing the emotions of millions of men and women.
You can see the victims in college football stadiums any
fall Saturday afternoon. Nevertheless, it should be
emphasized, that fascism has no existence independent
or apart from the socialization mechanisms (including
those of the militarized sports world) that systemati-
cally inculcate and perpetuate it. Ultimately it can have
no existence as a mass movement without the financial
and material support of the people who ultimately control those mechanisms,[2] and the material conditions
upon which this control is ultimately based.

About two decades ago, Lillian Smith, writing in her
book *Killers of the Dream,* advanced an explanation of
racism as having evolved as an invented rationale for
the white man's guilt-ridden domination of the black
male for the purpose of gaining access to the black female. And in order to further obscure the real nature of
what was historically a mass rape of black women by
white men, the white man now evinces a deep-seated
psychological fear that if the black man is not kept
down he will be after "our" women. This explanation
has recently been taken up by Eldridge Cleaver in

[2] Fascism is the ultimate weapon they resort to when
they can no longer suppress the workers' movements through
the orderly application of the so-called democratic process.
When this democratic process resulted in the election of progressive governments in Guatemala, Iran, and Brazil, and
threatened to do so in Greece, the CIA felt compelled to
install fascist governments. It was very similar in Italy and
Germany in the '20s and '30s. As the Left gathered strength
and threatened to take over the factories, Big Capital threw
its financial strength behind the führers of the Far Right. The
slogan was of course "Law and Order." In the United States
at the present time (unlike in Quebec and Northern Ireland)
it is still not quite necessary to physically smash the workers'
organizations of the Left, although in various elections (most
notably Agnew's speeches in the 1970 Congressional election) the "Law and Order" waters are constantly being
tested.

Soul on Ice. It is more or less the sexual dimension of the rough materialist view that sees racism as the ideology the white Western ruling class has evolved to rationalize its imperialist domination of colored peoples the world over—i.e., the White Man's Burden of civilizing the naked savages.

Clearly, the discussions of racism in terms of its hidden sexual motive force have much merit. They explain the incredible intensity of the hatred of the white race for the black. But they do not explain very well why white men regard white women as "our" women, or why there is such intense competition among males —whether white or black—for women. What the psychological explanation does, then, is attempt to reduce racism to sexism, and we should be content with reducing racism to sexism only if we regard sexism as somehow "natural" to the species.

But we have seen that the intensity of intra-male competition for women (and sexism generally) is directly proportional to the amount of sexual repression in society. And it was pointed out by Freud in *Civilization and Its Discontents* and *Beyond the Pleasure Principle* that this sexual repression imposed by society was intimately connected with the so-called Reality Principle or work ethic, by which Freud believed that sexual energy was canalized into the production of material and intellectual products of civilization. But what Freud did not emphasize was that the amount of sexual repression that would be necessary would be inversely related to the development of the means of production and the availability of material goods. Thus, in some direct sense the sexual repression required by society is proportional to the incomplete and unequal availability of material goods for the various classes, races, sexes, and nations.

The point is that the poisonous ideologies of elitism (especially class elitism), racism, sexism, and nationalism originate in the world-wide historical struggles for scarce resources. The word "scarce" in this context need not allude to a scarcity of what are called necessities but to the incomplete availability of the material goods most people regard as desirable for a fulfilling life. Granted there is a tendency toward conspicuous overconsumption, but this is partly because not everyone has the resources for this, and hence those who do acquire higher status. In this sense, elitism, nationalism, racism, and sexism are a function of consumerism, but one defined more quantitatively than qualitatively—say in terms of "our interests in the Third World," "I need a second car," etc. So the existence of these poisonous ideologies depends on people's acceptance of the bourgeois world view that defines happiness in terms of the *quantitative* accumulation of material goods, and their willingness to struggle against one another for these goods. The medium of this struggle is inter-group competition—and especially the ideology of competition—which originated historically on the battlefield and the sports field (the distinction between the two becoming more nebulous the further back we go into history). It was further intensified in the era of state monopoly capitalism, whose foreign side is global imperialism. For example, we have seen that in the team sports of its elite public schools, the British imperial ruling class learned the group solidarity that was the basis of its elitism, racism, sexism, and nationalism. The young sportsmen were subjected to a vicious regimen of heterosexual repression, so that the energy that might otherwise have gone into heterosexuality was now canalized into white (racist) male (sexist) British (nationalist) ruling class (elitism) chauvinism. Roughly the same has occurred in elite American prep schools.

As a general formula, we have:

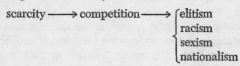

scarcity ——⟶ competition ——⟶ ⎰ elitism
                                 ⎱ racism
                                 ⎱ sexism
                                 ⎱ nationalism

and in this formula sports is a catalyst or socializer of competition, a competition tremendously intensified by the requirements of monopoly capitalism. It follows from this that the continuing cultural revolution in sports will weaken the ideology of competition which will, in turn, weaken the strength of elitism, racism, sexism, and nationalism.

Of course, ultimately we have to deal with the problem of scarce resources and the unequal distribution on a global scale of what resources there are, carried out by capitalism's class dictatorship and enforced by its state apparatus. Militarism is the most visible ideological arm of enforcement. And it might be thought that the domestic side of militarism arises out of a struggle for scarce resources between the military and civilian sectors of government, or possibly between those corporations producing mainly for military consumption and those producing mainly for civilian consumption. On the surface, this is true enough. But it is badly misleading to place the struggle for the production of military goods on the same footing as the struggle between classes, races, sexes, or nations for consumer goods and power. Since most military consumption is simply waste consumption, militarism (unlike class elitism, racism, sexism, and nationalism) is best seen as one of the main ways by which state monopoly capitalism *artificially* maintains the scarcity of available resources that is the underlying rationale of its class rule. So that in order to rid humanity of the scourges of elitism, racism, sexism, and nationalism the international proletariat (that 98-or-so per cent of the world's population who are wage workers and do not exercise control over people's means of production) must:

(1) smash the instruments of class rule (starting with the bourgeois state);

(2) eliminate waste production as part of the process of reorienting production around the satisfaction of human needs rather than profits;

(3) do away with scarcity entirely by establishing
    democratic (i.e., socialist) relations of produc-
    tion on a global scale.

It follows from this argument that the elitism, racism,
sexism, and nationalism which both distort present-day
monopoly capitalist sports, and are furthered by these
sports, will not be destroyed until we have made the
transition to socialism. And the growing cultural revolution in sports may well be an important step in this
direction.

Today, the movement in sports is escalating so
rapidly that it seems that not even jocks will be jocks.
Professional athletes like Bill Russell, Dave Meggyesy,
Chip Oliver, Brian Connacher, Johnny Sample, and
Bernie Parrish have written books attacking the sports
establishment. Others like Bill Bradley, Oscar Robertson, Duane Thomas, Alex Karras, George Sauer, Dave
Debusschere, Walter Beach, Joe Kapp and many others
have spoken out strongly. "Perhaps there is no room in
the world of sports these days for an athlete who has
an opinion on anything except his own sport," noted
Alex Karras when he was forced out of football. "I have
opinions. I think I am entitled to the same considerations as other human beings. That includes having the
right to express myself on something other than playing
defensive tackle. I will not change. If management
wants a player to be only a piece of flesh and treats
him as a member of the herd, then perhaps our mutual
best interests have been served" (by the waiver deal
that led to Karras' premature retirement).

When Philadelphia Eagles' coach Ed Khayat
ordered all his players to shave off their mustaches during the 1971 season, tackle Gary Pettigrew replied that,
"It just proves that when you play pro football for a
living that 1984 isn't really thirteen years away."
Middle-linebacker Timmy Rossovich added, "If this
team is so grooming conscious, why don't they ask

[owner] Leonard Tose to trim his eyebrows?" And even New York Jets' fullback Matt Snell was spotted by the *New York Post* (September 4, 1971) reading *The Soledad Brothers: Prison Letters of George Jackson.* "Pro sports isn't going to be able to cut them all out of the same cookie mold anymore," the *Post*'s columnist lamented. "This is depressing," said Snell of the death of Jackson. "This guy was in jail at age fifteen, and spent much of the next twelve years in solitary confinement. He was killed—shot down—a few weeks ago. Makes me realize how lucky I've been and that there's a lot going on out there."

Fortunately, there has been a lot going on *inside* the sports world as well. Perhaps the best symbol of it I know are some of the remarks attributed to big Ben Davidson, during the 1970 professional football players' strike when it was still uncertain whether all the teams would support the action. "I'm not making any threats," declared big Ben, one of the players' association's strongest supporters, "but you know how bitter some of these labor disputes get . . . Football is a rough game and it's conceivable that a team that went against us and all the other teams in the dispute might find itself suffering an unusual number of injuries." (The strike was eventually settled with the players reportedly winning $4.5 million in pension and insurance benefits over four years.) Similar strikes were undertaken by baseball players, and even baseball umpires. National Hockey League players held out for better contracts in unprecedented numbers. And professional basketball players threatened strike action to avoid a merger of the two leagues. The Nashville Dixie Flyers hockey team of the Eastern League unanimously boycotted a game in protest against bad conditions.

The college sports establishment was rocked even harder. Perhaps the clearest symbol here was the fate of Kent State grid coach Dave Puddington. After the 1970 National Guard shootings which left four of his students dead, the coach returned in the fall with the new motto, "Surging into the seventies on a positive note." It didn't last. Within three months, the coach had resigned because of the "negative attitude" toward football on campus. He was not alone. Coaches found themselves resigning or fired in unprecedented numbers. Even at little Coe College in Cedar Rapids, Iowa, a furor with the coaches erupted over hair styles. The coaches threatened to resign if their players were allowed to have long hair. The university president reminded them that times have changed, and henceforth grooming standards must change as well. So, the coaches quit. A year later, in another of those symbolic incidents, Steve Worster, who had just graduated as an All-American running back at the University of Texas was arrested in Hamilton, Ontario, and charged with possession of marijuana. The same year the quarterback of Navy's football team resigned from the Academy. The quality of the Army and Navy football teams declined disastrously in the late '60s because growing anti-war sentiment, even among high school footballers, made it extremely difficult to get promising recruits to enroll. And one week before the 1970 Army-Navy football game, Army's captain shocked the brass with the information that, "if you polled the football team and asked everybody about Vietnam, I think the feeling would be overwhelmingly in favor of getting out of there." Larry DiNardo, Notre Dame's All-American guard commented that the main impression he drew from his NCAA-sponsored trip to Vietnam was that "this war is a total waste."

Boycotts, strikes, disruptions, pickets, threatened resignations, and more took place in the athletic programs of more than two hundred American colleges and universities. Things got so turbulent in the fall of 1969 that *Sports Illustrated* appeared on the stands with a three-part article headed "The Desperate Coach." "The animals," says New York *Times* sports columnist Neil

Amdur (op. cit., p. 59), "are, it seems, finally out of their cages. Once contemptuously scorned as 'monkeys' and 'psychos' because of their reluctance to question established values, involved players at all levels have created their own movement for more personal freedom. Their targets are insensitive, autocratic coaches, owners, administrators, even a callous public." Sammy Goldberg, the decathlon star who was sacked from the team at the University of Kansas and later became Minister of Sport for the Youth International Party, noted, "Our major goal is to liberate the athlete from the status of performer and elevate him to the status of artist. No rational athlete should be happy with the way he is treated. Our policy is to end the abuses and cultural prostitution of sport by any means necessary." (Scott, op. cit., p. 195.) Will Hetzel, the basketball player for the University of Maryland, added:

> Playground games are so much more fun than college games. The people on the playground are playing primarily for the enjoyment of the physical activity, and that's what athletics should be about . . . Athletics can be such a beautiful thing. It's a shame to have to keep score. In fact, it's a shame to have to keep score on anything in life. (Ibid., p. 67.)

"All around the country," wrote University of Texas swimmer Frank J. Salzhandler in his school paper, "athletes are beginning to seek meaning and relevance behind the work and dedication they put into athletics. When these ideas are stunted by a coach who only wants a group of bodies to lead around by the nose, many athletes are left with no alternative but to speak out." Within twenty-four hours of the appearance of this article, Salzhandler was suspended from the team by Texas coach Bill Patterson, who insisted his "attitude was intolerable and not conducive to winning." (San Francisco *Examiner*, October 23, 1970, p. 50.)

And Lewis Leader, the former sports editor of Berkeley's *Daily Cal* wrote that the upheaval in college athletics seemed even to be reaching the press boxes. "It has been a custom for sports columnists and editors to be to the right of Genghis Khan politically, and to be behind Spiro Agnew in insight," he wrote. They probably sleep with "red, white, and blue covers." But things are changing. "It is no longer necessary to wear your American Legion or Veterans of Foreign Wars hat while writing sports. In many newspaper offices, it still helps, however." Still there is a little hope. Even some Establishment sportswriters like Leonard Shecter and Neil Amdur seem to have caught the little red bug.

For the movement of college athletes, as for the student movement as a whole, the high point of activity occurred during the May 1970 Cambodia invasion following the murders of students at Kent State and Jackson State. At the University of Southern California, athletes as a group met and issued the following statement:

> We, the overwhelming majority of California athletes, find that we can no longer live in the so-called "apolitical atmosphere" which has permeated the athletic community. We find it necessary now to voice our opposition to President Nixon's oppressive policies at home and abroad. We condemn United States activity in Southeast Asia and call for a unilateral withdrawal of all United States forces in Southeast Asia. Furthermore, we call for a reconstitution of American universities as centers against the war.

The wrestling team voted to boycott the National AAU wrestling championships. The track and tennis teams voted to wear black armbands and clenched fist protest symbols at forthcoming matches. Bob McLennan, captain of the track and field team, made a statement calling the invasion of Cambodia a betrayal of trust by the President, and threatening that, "The university will not return to normal until the war is ended." Mike

Mullan, representing the tennis team, noted that because of the extension of "the genocidal war in Southeast Asia" the tennis team would be wearing shirts with anti-war slogans in place of their usual uniforms in their next scheduled match. The football team at first announced that they would be boycotting spring practice, but later decided to resume them following various "discussions" with coaches. At the 1970 Heptagonal Track and Field Championships, teams representing the eight Ivy League schools issued a statement condemning the continuation of the war, "the repression of the Black Panther Party and people of radical disposition in general." They added that, "as athletes and track men, we understand that our sport is not and must never become a hide-out from our basic responsibilities as human beings." Presumably in order to preserve the hide-out, the Army and Navy teams were quickly ordered to withdraw from the meet. In the meantime, as an even more forceful anti-war protest, another forty-five Ivy League track-and-field men boycotted the meet entirely. At Columbia (where only thirteen months earlier jocks had blockaded and beat up SDSers) the baseball, track, tennis, and golf teams voted to cancel all competition, and eighty-five footballers endorsed a petition calling for a national student strike. It seemed that on this campus at least, last year's fascists might become this year's socialists. "Once we heard that the athletes and pompom girls had joined the demonstrations," commented a Nixon administration official at the height of it all, "we knew we were in trouble."

Meanwhile in the United States, Britain, Ireland, Australia, and New Zealand anti-apartheid demonstrators stormed onto playing fields in an attempt to break up cricket, rugby, golf, or tennis matches involving South Africans. In England the 1970 South African springboks cricket tour had to be cancelled in the face of such protests. (The London branch of the British National Union of Journalists had earlier voted that if the tour were held, they would refuse to report it.) In Ireland the protest demonstrations against the springboks rugby tour were directed by the mainstream of the trade union movement. The cricket, rugby, golf, and tennis bureaucracies in England particularly have not been unknown to be dominated by individuals who have huge investments in apartheid-operated South African industry, and the anti-apartheid demonstrations seemed a good way of imposing the public's more progressive morality on the Lords of the Pitch. (Unfortunately, there were still serious differences of opinion about this. In Leicester, during the 1969 rugby tour, traditionalist "fans," including many off-duty policemen, got themselves "deputized" into Right-wing vigilante groups to "protect" the match against Left-wing anti-apartheid demonstrators. A vicious battle then erupted in the stands—with the police giving full support to the Right-wingers—which seemed to mirror the struggle between fascism and socialism in society generally.) However, the willingness of some fans to undertake protest demonstrations and sit-ins to get their view across to the players, boded a breakdown in the barrier between the realms of players and fans, which is at the very heart of elitist-oriented sports.

In the United States the barrier also came under strong attack at scores of colleges where students voted to cut off or cut down funds for elite intercollegiate teams, and use the money instead to promote intramural sports in which a wide campus cross section might participate. Throughout the '60s, even in the military services, pressures continually built up to downgrade elite varsity-type teams in favor of more intramural type arrangements in which a far larger group of servicemen could compete. There were also demonstrations from civil rights and black nationalist supporters about the inadequate numbers of black cheerleaders, and demonstrations from women's liberationists about whether *there should be any cheerleaders*. At

UCLA, a year after the Watts riots, the title of head yell leader was won by black anti-war activist Eddie Anderson. He promptly introduced a rendition of "Bomb Around the Clock" (a take-off on Bill Haley's "Rock Around the Clock"). Also included were cheers dedicated to white coeds who were dating black guys, and other assorted plugs for black power. "How big is the Big Game?" demanded the head yell leader. "How big is it when, during the other six days in the week, there is the Big Draft, the Big War and the Big Election? We need to have the kids indentify with something more than just the football team. Being rah-rah for the football team is not going to get that identity."

But maybe the gathering cultural revolution in sports will. There is, of course, no such thing as jock liberation, apart from the more general cultural revolution in society as a whole, apart from black liberation, women's liberation, the student's and worker's control movements. The cultural revolution in sports is nothing more nor less than the reflection of these larger movements in society as a whole. It can be no more successful than their combined effectiveness. In fact, though they are all elements of it, it is extremely unlikely that there can be black liberation, women's liberation, meaningful student power, or jock liberation, without world-wide human liberation. No doubt these movements and the national liberation struggles in Vietnam, Northern Ireland, Quebec, and so on, are all different fronts of the world-wide human liberation struggle, which to achieve final victory may yet require what amounts to global socialist revolution. To one degree or another, it is already underway in every country of the world. Our various domestic movements, including the upheavals in the sports world, are but one reflection of it. The stakes of this "game" are extremely high. The oppressed peoples of the neo-colonial world will certainly not wait. Our rulers here are rapidly militarizing our society and our sports in preparation for the future

Vietnam wars in which they will expect us to put down
our brothers abroad with our own blood. Things cannot stay the same. Society, and its sports are polarizing
rapidly. We still have the choice of either fighting to
preserve the neo-colonialist profits of our bosses or fighting together with the peoples of the neo-colonies to
abolish the system of bosses entirely. As Dave Meggyesy puts it:

> You know, it seems to me that we're at a critical point
> in our history as a nation, a critical point in our cul-
> ture. And it's pretty much come down to, in the last
> five years, the death culture versus the life culture.
> The death culture has as its key notes, competition
> and emphasis on product, which is an emphasis on
> winning, score those touchdowns. It's an emphasis on
> military victories, not humane rational solutions. And
> the life culture is trying to say something else. It's
> saying, instead of competition, let's think about co-
> operation, let's think about working together . . .
>
> So to the athletes, all of whom are getting ripped
> off at the university level, get yourselves together.
> And for the rest of you, understand why football
> exists in this country and understand your relation-
> ship to the institutions . . . which make you less
> free and alienate you from your brothers and sisters.
> Because a shit-storm's coming down in this country,
> and it's a struggle between the forces of life and the
> forces of death. WE ARE THE GENERATION THAT'S
> CRUCIAL, BECAUSE WE ARE RESPONSIBLE FOR MAKING
> THE REVOLUTION, AND BRINGING INTO BEING THE
> VISION. (From "Take Me Out of the Ball Game";
> broadcast over National Educational Television,
> March 15, 1971.)

In the last analysis, in the sports world, as in the
world as a whole, it will be socialism or fascism, global
human liberation or barbarism.

Supplemental Readings

This reading list was prepared by Jack and Micki Scott of the Institute for the Study of Sport and Society (ISSS). It should, of course, be noted that neither the author nor the ISSS necessarily agree with the ideas expressed in all of these books. Books and articles marked with an asterisk, however, are works that are critical of the sports establishment's world view.

Amdur, Neil. *The Fifth Down.* New York: Coward McCann & Geoghegan, 1971.

Axthelm, Pete. "The Angry Black Athlete," *Newsweek* (July 15, 1968), pp. 56–60.

———. *The City Game.* New York: Harper's Magazine Press, 1970.

Bannister, Roger. *The Four-Minute Mile*. New York: Dodd, Mead, 1963.

*Barnes, LaVerne. *The Plastic Orgasm*. Toronto: McClelland & Stewart, 1971.

Beisser, Arnold R. *The Madness in Sport*. New York: Appleton-Century-Crofts, 1967.

Benagh, Jim. "Case Study of a College Coach," *Sport* (July 1970), pp. 32–35, 74–77.

Berkow, Ira. Five-part series on the state of intercollegiate football. Available from the Newspaper Enterprise Assoc., 230 Park Ave., New York, 1970.

Bouton, Jim. "A Mission in Mexico City," *Sport* (August 1969), pp. 64–65.

Brasher, Christopher, ed. *The Road to Rome*. London: William Kimber, 1960.

Chataway, Chris. "The Future of the Olympics." *The Road to Rome*, ed. Chris Brasher. London: William Kimber, 1960.

*Edwards, Harry. *The Revolt of the Black Athlete*. New York: The Free Press, 1969.

Farr, Finis. *Black Champion*. London: Macmillan and Co., Ltd., 1964.

*Flood, Curt. *The Way It Is*. New York: Trident Press, 1970.

Gilbert, B. Three-part series on drugs in sports. *Sports Illustrated* (June 23, 30; July 7, 1969), pp. 64–72, 30–42, 30–35.

Goodhart, Philip, M.P., and Chataway, Christopher. *War Without Weapons*. London: W. H. Allen, 1968.

Green, P. W. "Shamateurism," *Athletics Weekly* (October 7, 1961), p. 3.

*Hart, Marie. "Sport: Women Sit in the Back of the Bus," *Psychology Today* (October 1971), pp. 64–66.

*Hoffman, Abigail. "Super-Jock in Decline: Liberating

Sport from Sexist Stereotypes," *Canadian Dimension* (August 1971), pp. 41–42.

Izenberg, J. "Pro Football's Lily White Position: The Conspiracy Against Black Quarterbacks," *True* (February 1969), pp. 32–34, 78–79, 82.

Jackson, Myles. "College Football Has Become a Losing Business," *Fortune* (December 1962), pp. 119–21.

Johnson, Jack. *Jack Johnson Is a Dandy*. New York: New American Library, 1970.

Kidd, Bruce. "Canada's 'National' Sport," *Close to the 49th Parallel,* ed. Ian Lumsden. Toronto: University of Toronto Press, 1970.

Lucas, Bob. *Black Gladiator*. New York: Dell, 1970.

*Meggyesy, Dave. *Out of Their League*. Berkeley: Ramparts, 1970.

Melnick, M. S. "Footballs and Flower Power," *Jopher* (October 1969), p. 32.

Miller, Arthur. *Death of a Salesman*. New York: Viking Press, 1958.

Mitchell, Brian, ed. *Today's Athlete*. London: Pelham Books, 1970.

*Oliver, Chip. *High for the Game*. New York: William Morrow, 1971.

*Olsen, Jack. *The Black Athlete: A Shameful Story*. New York: Time-Life Books, 1968.

*Padwe, Sandy. "Big-Time College Football Is on the Skids," *Look* (September 22, 1970), pp. 66–69.

*Parrish, Bernie. *They Call It a Game*. New York: Dial Press, 1971.

Peterson, Robert W. *Only the Ball Was White*. Englewood Cliffs: Prentice-Hall, 1970.

Rapoport, Roger. "Pro Football's Dropouts," *Sport* (September 1970), pp. 54–55, 92–96.

Russell, Bill. *Go Up for Glory*. New York: Coward McCann, 1966.

*———. "Success Is a Journey," *Sports Illustrated* (July 8, 1970), pp. 81–93.

*Scott, Jack. *The Athletic Revolution.* New York: The
    Free Press, 1971.
*———. "It's Not How You Play the Game, but What
    Pill You Take," New York *Times Magazine* (Oc-
    tober 17, 1971), pp. 40–41, 106–12, 114.
*———. "The White Olympics," *Ramparts* (May 1968),
    pp. 54–61.
*———, and Edwards, Harry. "After the Olympics:
    Buying off Protest," *Ramparts* (November
    1969), pp. 16–21.
*Shecter, Leonard. *The Jocks.* New York: Bobbs-
    Merrill, 1969.
Sillitoe, Alan. *The Loneliness of the Long-Distance
    Runner.* New York: New American Library,
    1959.
*Tunis, John R. *$port$: Heroics and Hysterics.* New
    York: John Day, 1928.
Underwood, J. "The Desperate Coach," *Sports Illus-
    trated* (August 25; September 1, 8, 1969).
*Wolf, Dave. *Foul! Connie Hawkins, Schoolyard Star,
    Exile, NBA Superstar.* New York: Holt, Rinehart
    and Winston, 1972.

Index